PRAISE ABOUT THE AUTHOR

"JC emulated grace and it was demonstrated not only through what he wrote and spoke, but how he lived his life."

KRISSIE BENSON

Clinical Therapist, Stronghold Counseling Services

"Perhaps the best metaphor to describe JC comes from his experience in coaching basketball. As coach of Stronghold, JC understood the stage of development and strengths of each of his players. He nurtured them, invested in them, and attended to them, and in return they trusted him, grew in confidence, and improved their skills. JC enjoyed watching his players—his clients, his supervisees, and his clinicians—be transformed, especially when they surprised themselves by becoming the players they didn't know they could be."

SUSAN TERVEEN

Clinical Therapist, Stronghold Counseling Services

"JC Chambers was many things: a therapist, a mentor, a father and husband, an artist, a businessman, a teacher, a friend. Most importantly, he was a man who believed wholeheartedly in the power of Christ's grace. His greatest legacy is in the thousands of people who have found Christ's grace for themselves thanks to his guidance."

MATT MERRITT

Co-author of The Art of Kid Whispering

"I heard when I was in my early twenties, "You can't soar with the eagles when you are surrounded with turkeys," and, "You don't find eagles in flocks, you find them one at a time." I have found eagles throughout my life, but JC was my main eagle. I owe everything to JC Chambers and will be forever in his debt."

EARL WITT

Clinical Therapist, Stronghold Counseling Services

"I have had the honor of being JC's colleague for over 20 years. JC's lasting legacy is the grace extended to the hurting individuals "doing" life. He created a safe place to experience grace through his presence, personality, and language. JC was dedicated to his understanding of God, his family, his colleagues, and his community."

GARY HOFMAN

Clinical Therapist, Stronghold Counseling Services

Freely

TRANSFORMING LIVES THROUGH THE EYES OF GRACE

THRONE
PUBLISHING GROUP

A THIRTY DAY DEVOTIONAL

Freely

TRANSFORMING LIVES THROUGH THE EYES OF GRACE

JC CHAMBERS & THE STRONGHOLD CREW

Cover Design: Carley Chambers - Internal Layout Design: Amy Gehling - Lead Writer: JC Chambers and The Stronghold Crew - Editor: Noah Sundstrom - Proofing Editor: Amy Rollinger - Publishing Manager: Brooke Brown

Throne Publishing Group: 2329 N Career Ave #241, Sioux Falls, SD 57107
ThronePG.com

TABLE OF CONTENTS

DEDICATION

In loving memory of a man who meant so much to so many. Husband, Dad, Papa, Son, Brother, Boss, Mentor, Coach, and Friend. You are so missed. You left your marks of grace on all of our lives.

You will always be remembered.

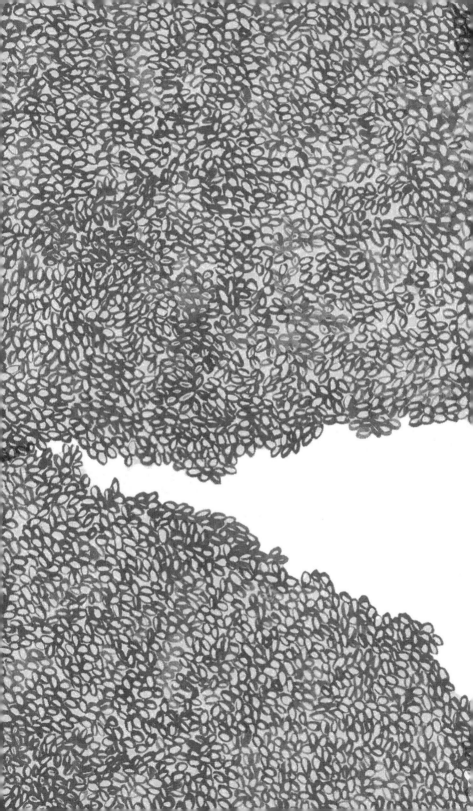

Foreword

FOREWORD

It has been said that the person writing the foreword of a book should show "social proof" of their connection to the author. I was married to Dr. Jamie (JC) Chambers for over 34 years. We have three daughters, two sons-in-love, a new grandson, and one very busy counseling agency between us. I'd say that is adequate proof of how well I knew JC Chambers.

Everywhere we went, other people also knew him, knew of him, or wanted to know him. Everyone wanted a piece of him and he freely gave them one. Sometimes that annoyed me. Sometimes that cost me and our girls our time with him. To us he was just a husband and a dad. But that's who he was. He gave people that and more. He freely offered them hope, acceptance, a window into their deepest hurts, and, most of all, he freely offered them grace. Grace was the filter he used to point people to the transforming love and freedom he had found in Christ as a young college sophomore in a small Kansas town.

I like to say that JC ran Stronghold Counseling Services and I ran everything else. It was a partnership that worked for us and was born out of a love for our family and a commitment we made to our marriage to stick together even when the going got rough. I never expected how drastically life would change on a sunny summer day in July, 2018. His unexpected death changed everything.

He had asked me several months prior to his death if I wanted to write a devotional for the "project" he was putting together for Stronghold's 25th Anniversary celebration. True to my usual form, I declined, probably rather strongly. So here's the irony, right? Not only do I now have an entry in the book, I'm writing this foreword, and I'm learning to run the business that he devoted his life to. I hope to do it in a way that honors his legacy and continues to provide care for this broken world in which we live.

This devotional book was the last project he was working on before he died so suddenly. I only learned about it at the visitation when Jeremy, owner of Throne Publishing, handed me a simple folder with the manuscript contained inside. He said to me, "I thought you might like to have this." Many people have come together in a big hurry to put this book in your hands in time for our 25th Anniversary. I owe a lot to my girls and family, the staff at Stronghold (especially Gena, who has basically been running the ship the last 6 weeks), the people at Throne Publishing, and, most of all, the many people who have freely given back to me such love and grace, support and prayers. I hope that you are encouraged by these devotionals written lovingly by present and former Stronghold staff and family. JC would want you to know that God loves you for free—no strings attached. He even likes you and wants to get to know you! No matter who you are or what you think you've done or haven't done, it's not about you; it's all about Him.

God's grace is freely given to you. Your charge is to freely give it away.

— *Lorri Chambers*

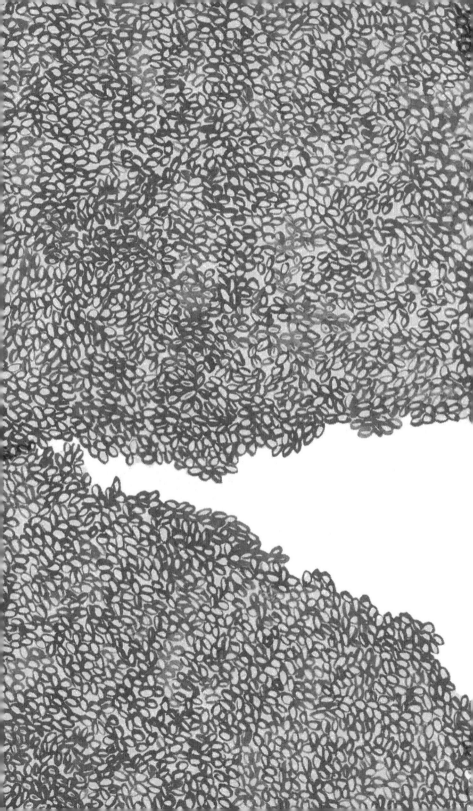

Introduction

INTRODUCTION

When people hear I was JC's office manager for almost 20 years, they use these words to describe him: brother, father, son. That tells you the character of the man this book is dedicated to. I was blessed to call him all three. He was my father when he was encouraging and challenging me. And he was my brother when we argued or bounced ideas off each other. And he was my son when I was picking up after him (he always left his stuff in my office!). Of course, the most important title he earned and gave was friend. JC was a true friend when he was reassuring or comforting and giving me confidence in myself.

JC's last breath here was his first breath in heaven. When he closed his eyes on earth, he opened them up to glory, pavements of gold, mansions, and the loving eyes of a Savior. And that

Savior spoke the words in Luke 19 to him: *"Well done, my good servant!"*

JC sowed many seeds. He sowed seeds in his family, in his staff, in those who walked into Stronghold (whether they were his clients or not), on the basketball court, and in the lives of just about everyone he crossed paths with. Those seeds were obvious in the 25,000-plus views, shares, and posts that were on social media within a week of his passing. His desire was for each of us to know God likes us. A concept even greater than God's love for us. His desire was what God wants for all the world, "None to perish and all to have the gift of eternal life."

This book has been put together using some of JC's own words, writings, and drawings. Included with his work are the works of his family and his staff. JC influenced and coached each of us to be a better version of ourselves, so we could pour that into the world around us. It's like that principle in science, "In physics, the law of conservation of energy means that energy can neither be created nor destroyed; rather, it can only be transformed/transferred from one form to another." Energy has been transformed and transferred.

Together we get to carry, grow, transform, and transfer this legacy. We will personalize it, just as Coach JC empowered and wanted us to. May this book also empower you to touch and change the lives around you.

— *Gena Tarrell, Office Manager*

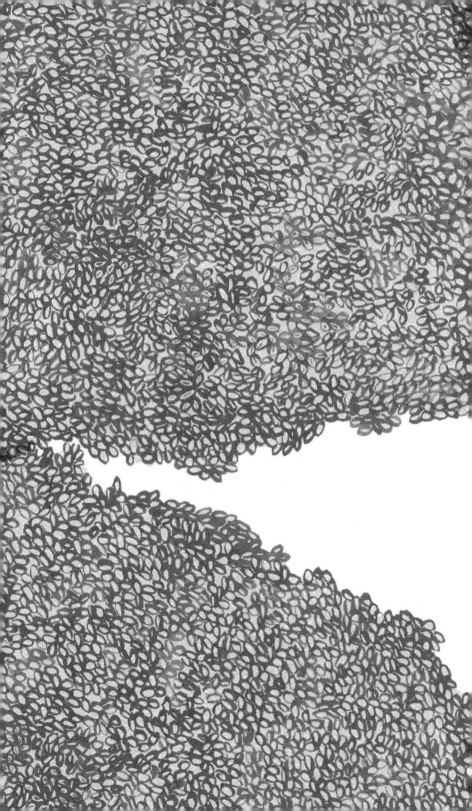

Day 1: Freely He Gives

"For I am convinced that neither death nor life, neither angels nor demons, neither the present nor the future, nor any powers, neither height nor depth, nor anything else in all creation, will be able to separate us from the love of God that is in Christ Jesus our Lord."

— Romans 8:38-39 (NIV) —

FREELY HE GIVES

This is the verse my mom chose for her funeral. At the time, I didn't know it was one of her favorite verses, but then things from my parents' lives began to stand out and it made sense. I remember the day of their 40th anniversary celebration when I was still in high school. I scraped their car on another car that was in the driveway. I was determined not to tell them until after the party, to not put a cloud on the day. As I was getting ready, I started to cry and out it came. But they told me, "It's a car, we will check it out tomorrow." There was another time when I had something to tell them that I was ashamed of, and they told me, "It's all in a lifetime. There's good, there's bad, but it's all in a lifetime." And there was the time I asked my dad why he had done something so above and beyond for me, and he told me, "You're my kid." No other explanation was necessary. There were plenty of other times when my parents reflected God's love. God's love tells us, "You're my kid." Once I give up and give in to Him, I'm His kid. There is nothing more I need to be or do.

Abba, Daddy, I only want to thank and praise you! Amen.

Dig deeper: Romans 8:31-39

— *Gena Tarrell, Office Manager*

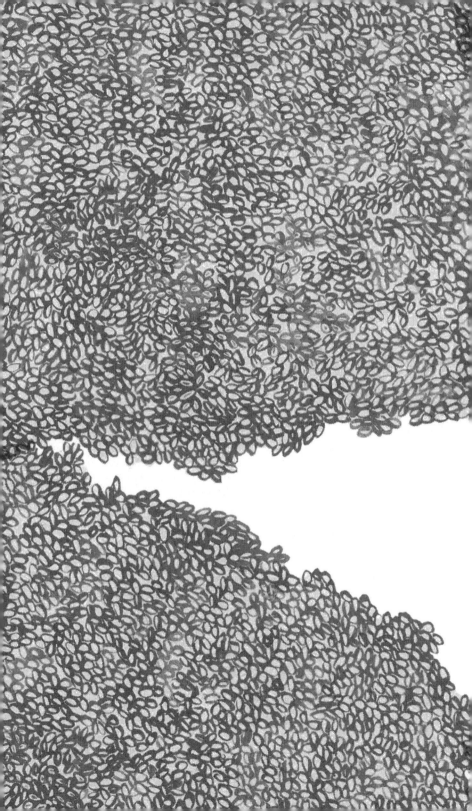

Day 2: Freely He Died

FREELY

"But God demonstrates his own love for us in that the Messiah died on our behalf while we were still sinners."

— *Romans 5:8 (CJB)* —

FREELY HE DIED

In *Today in The World* on April 1, 1992, there was a story titled "Each Chaplain Gave Up His Life Jacket:"

"Boarding the SS Dorchester on a dreary winter day in 1943 were 903 troops and four chaplains, including Moody alumnus Lt. George Fox. World War II was in full swing, and the ship was headed across the icy North Atlantic where German U-boats lurked. At 12:00 in the morning of February 3, a German torpedo ripped into the ship. "She's going down!" the men cried, scrambling for lifeboats. A young GI crept up to one of the chaplains. "I've lost my life jacket," he said. "Take this," the chaplain said, handing the soldier his jacket. Before the ship sank, each chaplain gave his life jacket to another man. The heroic chaplains then linked arms and lifted their voices in prayer as the Dorchester went down. Lt. Fox and his fellow pastors were awarded posthumously the Distinguished Service Cross."

Those pastors made the ultimate sacrifice for a noble cause. They all understood the honor and value of delivering servicemen to battle. They understood the sacrifices those men were about to make. They understood the value of having soldiers arrive at their destination. Dying for our servicemen makes all kinds of sense.

But Jesus freely gave His life, not for the noble, not for the honorable, not for the righteous, but for the sinner, for the unrighteous, and for the reprobate. Our Lord gave His life for those who were distant, who were alien, who were hostile, and who were enemies of His way. Most people wouldn't make a sacrifice for those kinds of people, but representing His Father, Jesus freely did that for us.

As we continue to read in Romans, the passage further teaches that love is best demonstrated by someone giving up their life for the greater purpose of others, and the "others" includes enemies, jerks, reprobates, and criminals, not just good people.

That kind of love does three things. The love of God shown to us through Christ insulates us from God's wrath and from God's judgement, so we no longer have to live in fear. The love of God shown to us through the death of Christ also reconciles us with the Father. As we continue to read in Romans, Paul tells us that nothing can separate us from the love of God. In other words, it restores our relationship and creates relational permanence. And thirdly, the love of God shown to us through the death of Christ secures us. It not only secures our future, it gives us a secure base to live from in the here and now. So, the amazing thing about love shown to us through Christ's life and death is that it insulates us from wrath, reconciles us with the Father, and secures our relationship with God forever.

Father, we praise you for the action that was completed by your Son in His life and death on the cross. And we thank you for the love that you demonstrated to us because it reconciles, insulates and secures us. Help us to remember and remain in that love as we live our lives here on Earth.

Dig deeper: Romans 5:6-11 and Romans 8:31-39

— *Dr. JC Chambers, Co-founder (1959-2018)*

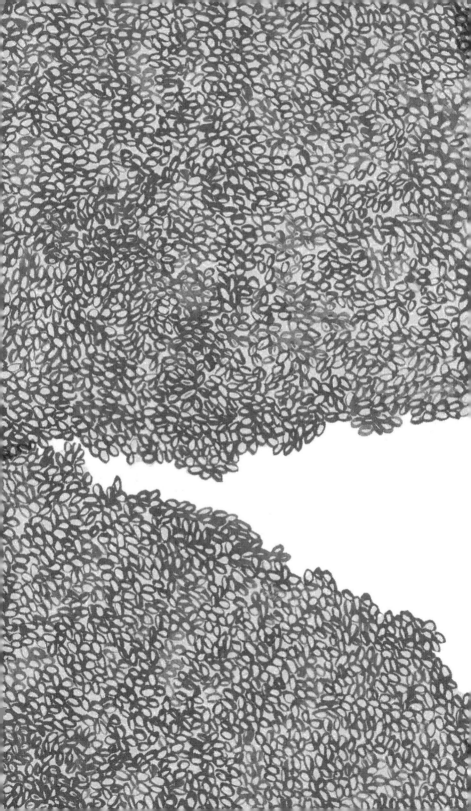

Day 3: Freely He Suffered

"While he lived on earth, anticipating death, Jesus cried out in pain and wept in sorrow as he offered up priestly prayers to God. Because he honored God, God answered him. Though he was God's Son, he learned trusting-obedience by what he suffered, just as we do. Then, having arrived at the full stature of his maturity and having been announced by God as high priest in the order of Melchizedek, he became the source of eternal salvation to all who believingly obey him."

— Hebrews 5:7-10 (MSG) —

"Do you see what this means—all these pioneers who blazed the way, all these veterans cheering us on? It means we'd better get on with it. Strip down, start running—and never quit! No extra spiritual fat, no parasitic sins. Keep your eyes on Jesus, who both began and finished this race we're in. Study how he did it. Because he never lost sight of where he was headed—that exhilarating finish in and with God—he could put up with anything along the way: Cross, shame, whatever. And now he's there, in the place of honor, right alongside God. When you find yourselves flagging in your faith, go over that story again, item by item, that long litany of hostility he plowed through. That will shoot adrenaline into your souls!"

— *Hebrews 12:1-3 (MSG)* —

FREELY HE SUFFERED

NBC NEWS headline reads: **"Firewalk Participants Defend Tony Robbins After Dozens Treated for Burns"**

"Participants at a Dallas event where about 30 followers of motivational speaker Tony Robbins were burned while walking on hot coals defended Robbins on Sunday, saying the incident had been vastly overblown."

The story goes on to say, "7000 participants have successfully completed the fire walk over 35 year of doing the event." Those folks probably paid several hundred dollars to attend the 3 or 4 day workshop to sit under the teaching of Anthony Robbins. The climax of that event would have been the fire walk.

When Jesus came to earth, He knew a couple of the fiery coals He would be walking on would be suffering, sorrow, shame, hostility, and humiliation on the cross. But He came anyway, and He freely gave up the privilege and position of being our God. He freely chose to join us, to suffer, to show us what the Father's love looks like.

In a day and age when we are fighting to gain or keep privilege, when we read about a God who was willing to give all that up, we should ask ourselves, "what was God's purpose in doing so?" The answer is to show us His love for us through His Son. As a consequence, He asked us "To sit under His teaching, to listen under His teaching." In other words, we are called "to be obedient" unto the same privilege of humiliation, shame, hostility, suffering, and sorrow at the cost of our own crosses. But we have the promise that we will indeed be with Him in heaven and have a place at the right and left side of the Father.

Father, help us to remember that salvation was your idea, that the plan to send your Son was your idea, and that the Son's willingness to come was motivated by love and a desire to help us understand your idea. Help us to firmly believe that Jesus came, suffered, lived, and endured a life here on earth for us to see what the Father's love looks like, and for us to be able to sit with Him when it's all said and done. Help us to remember that Jesus freely chose this because of the love He and the Father have for us. Help us to remember that His love for us is what motivated salvation.

— *Dr. JC Chambers, Co-founder (1959-2018)*

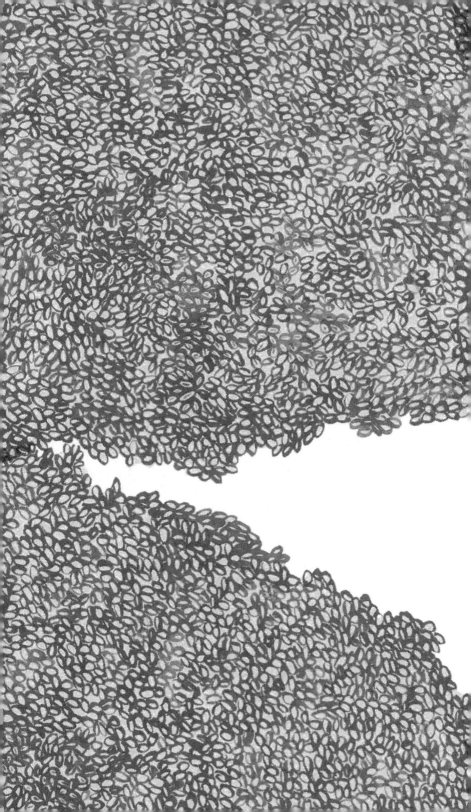

Day 4: Freely He Bestows Mercy

"As Jesus passed on from there, he saw a man named Matthew sitting at the customs post. He said to him, "Follow me." And he got up and followed him. While he was at table in his house, many tax collectors and sinners came and sat with Jesus and his disciples. The Pharisees saw this and said to his disciples, "Why does your teacher eat with tax collectors and sinners?" He heard this and said, 'Those who are well do not need a physician, but the sick do. Go and learn the meaning of the words, 'I desire mercy, not sacrifice.' I did not come to call the righteous but sinners.' Then the disciples of John approached him and said, 'Why do we and the Pharisees fast [much], but your disciples do not fast?' Jesus answered them, 'Can the wedding guests mourn as long as the bridegroom is with them? The days will come when the bridegroom is taken away from them, and then they will fast. No one patches an old cloak with a piece of unshrunken cloth, for its fullness pulls away from the cloak and the tear gets worse. People do not put new wine into old wineskins. Otherwise the skins burst, the wine spills out, and the skins are ruined. Rather, they pour new wine into fresh wineskins, and both are preserved.'"

— Matthew 9:9-17 (NABRE) —

FREELY HE BESTOWS MERCY

Meet Noelle, a beautiful, amazing, and loving woman, whose mantra was "love and peace." Her philosophy of living life was to live in companionship with others. She believed that "no one should walk home alone." This translated into a life that was lived for others boldly, brightly, and with creativity. She shone.

She had just moved to El Dorado, CA to escape what she saw as an increase in violent crime in Sacramento where she had been living. On January 6, she and her friend went to a favorite pub and eatery to celebrate their birthdays. Leaving the establishment just after midnight, a paroled felon accosted them, demanding cash and their car. As Noelle ran to return to the safety of the building, he fatally gunned her down and stole her car. Her friend made it to safety around the corner as the convict fled. In the months that followed, in their profound loss and depth of sadness, Noelle's devastated parents were invited to pursue the death penalty for the man.

Meet St. Matthew. Prior to heeding Jesus' call to "Follow me," he may have looked like you and me. He worked for the Roman administrators collecting taxes and likely spent his days extorting funds from his (former) friends, family, and his Jewish brothers and sisters. Taxes in themselves were likely to be oppressive, and yet, in all likelihood, Matthew (like other tax collectors of the time) charged a little extra to pad his own pocket. St. Matthew behaved as a thief, traitor, and a sinner. His life was about to change, though, when he encountered the merciful gaze of Jesus. It transformed him. The mercy of Jesus does that—it transforms. Jesus, in front of Matthew, doesn't vocalize the errors of his ways. Jesus responds to his thirst and desire, by saying, "Follow me." Jesus sees St. Matthew's thirst for something more and lifts St. Matthew out of his isolation, loneliness, insecurity, and self-doubt created by his attempts to meet his needs by his own abilities. What was in that gaze that led St. Matthew to leave all that he had, all that he spent his life working toward? I suggest it was the gaze of mercy.

The gospel story goes on to describe Jesus sharing His life with other tax collectors and sinners. He spent His time with others who lived in a marginalized way. Their humanity was reduced to nothingness, possibly left and discarded along the way, but Jesus showed them love and companionship, nonetheless. Jesus enters into our humanity in the same way. He entered that home in St. Matthew's time, and He does the same in our lives.

Mercy has a name—Jesus. Jesus calls you and me, as He did to St. Matthew, saying "follow me." In His mercy, in who He (Christ) is, He calls us (thieves, traitors, addicts, gossipers, sinners) to Himself. His merciful gaze responds to our needs. His gaze of love, mercy, and compassion transforms our doubt into certainty, our isolation into community, and our poverty into the riches of His kingdom.

Mercy is who Jesus is. Freely, Jesus bestows (gives) Himself to us. Jesus is the merciful love of the Father to you and to me.

In the event of St. Matthew, the Pharisees began to peck at Jesus' disciples by trying to discredit Jesus' lack of observance for the law. Jesus intervened and stated, *"Those who are well do not need a physician, but the sick do."* Jesus further challenges the Pharisees (who in their attachment to the law are unable to experience the merciful gaze offered to them) and provides direction. He advised them to go learn the meaning of *"I desire mercy, not sacrifice. I have not come to call the righteous, but sinners."*

Mercy is an interior (heart) disposition of love with an exterior action when suffering is encountered. Jesus continually and freely bestows His mercy on us. I dare say I don't think Jesus desires us to reduce His love and mercy to an empty ideology or set of laws (like the Pharisees) that is not an expression of His presence. It is the certainty of His presence that frees us to leave our "customs post" as St. Matthew did and heed Jesus' call to follow Him. It is the certainty of His continual gaze of mercy that frees us to live in His presence, even in the weakness and limitations of our humanity.

As Jesus calls, "Follow me," He asks us to also freely bestow mercy on our brothers and sisters. He doesn't ask us to begin at the place of our neighbor's errors. He asks us to respond to their needs, such as their thirst, longing, fear, loneliness, isolation, etc. He asks us to be His presence, His light in their darkness. This could be done through deed, word, and prayer.

Meet Noelle's mom, Lori. At the sentencing hearing, in front of God, family, the judge, friends, and the felon who killed her generous daughter, Lori made a victim impact statement. She said, in part, "The Bible tells us you must forgive 7 times 70. We choose not to pursue the death penalty because one unnatural death is one death too many." She bravely continued to address the defendant: "We also pray that you ask forgiveness from Noelle. For had you just asked, she would have given you a ride, offered you direction, or simply guided you to help. No, you had to take the best thing your life had in that moment— Noelle." She finished by saying, "We cannot condemn him, for the final judgment isn't ours. We miss her. May God have mercy on your soul."

Meet Noelle's family. They are living mercy for the man who murdered their beloved daughter and sister. They make an act of mercy toward him everyday as they pray for Christ's strength and mercy to forgive him. They embrace the man who shattered their lives, through their prayers. Their certainty in Christ provides them with the freedom to follow Jesus and freely bestow mercy. They embody words said by Fr. Luigi Guissani: "You stress the positive (all the good that Christ has done through the loss of this woman) despite all of its limitations (living with a hole in one's heart), and you leave everything else to the Father's mercy.

Heavenly Father, we praise you for your Son, Jesus, who is mercy. We thank you for His life, death, and resurrection that saves us and keeps us in your gaze. Help us to receive your mercy. Transform us from tax collectors into disciples who extend your mercy to others. Provide us with opportunities to freely give what we have freely received—mercy.

— *Teresa Henrickson, Clinical Therapist, Yankton Stronghold*

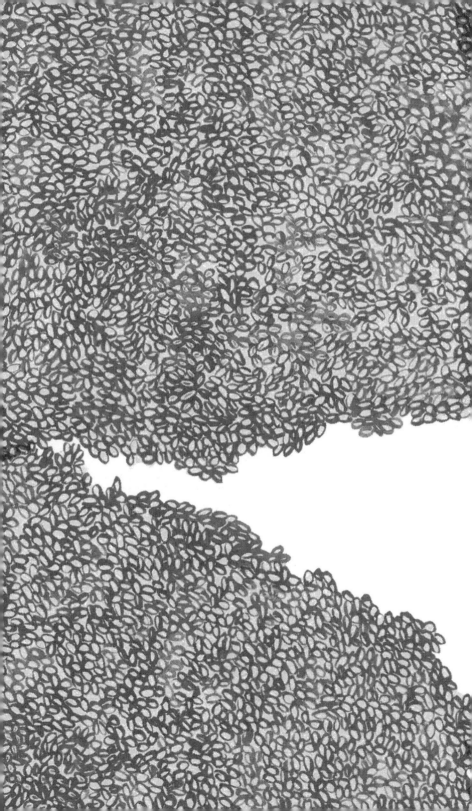

Day 5: Freely He Extends Righteousness (Part One)

FREELY

"I do not set aside the grace of God, for if righteousness could be gained through the law, Christ died for nothing."

— *Galatians 2:21 (NIV)* —

DAY

5

FREELY HE EXTENDS RIGHTEOUSNESS

(PART ONE)

"God helps those who help themselves." "God doesn't give you more than you can handle." Those are just a few of the sayings that I have heard in my lifetime that put the responsibility on me. We are taught and driven to work, provide, meet the mark, wanting to hear the "attaboy/girl," and to know that we have "arrived." Proverbial sentiments are alive and well in the world and in the church, such as do this, don't do that, can you help with one more thing? Or have I got a job for you! What we receive from these "tasks" are our due reward/payment for the effort we have put in. Striving for paychecks, bartering, dealmaking, and do-it-yourself are common mindsets for those who don't want to owe anything to anyone. When we have those mindsets, they leave us exhausted, wanting, and running around with a hole in our emotional bucket, never finding fullness.

The Law was given to meet the requirement of righteousness, but Jesus came to fulfill the Law and be our righteousness. Faith in Christ is where our righteousness is found, not in our to-do lists or constant striving. When we believe with our actions, as Abraham did, our faith *"Is credited as righteousness,"* Romans 4:5 (NIV). Righteousness is a gift given to us. It's a gift that has nothing to do about us, but it has everything to do with the heart of the giver, Jesus Christ. The Law brings condemnation and death, but through Jesus we find life and righteousness. "I have been crucified with Christ and I no longer live, but Christ lives in me," Galatians 2:20 (NIV). Christ died to (freely) give us His righteousness. It's not received through our efforts (do's and don'ts), but through the gift of grace.

Thank you, Jesus, that you have come to fulfill the Law and be our righteousness. May your Spirit show itself through us, so that we may reflect the glory that is only found in you, and point to you and not ourselves. Amen.

Dig deeper: Romans 4:4-8 and Galatians 2:19-21

— *Earl Witt, Clinical Therapist*

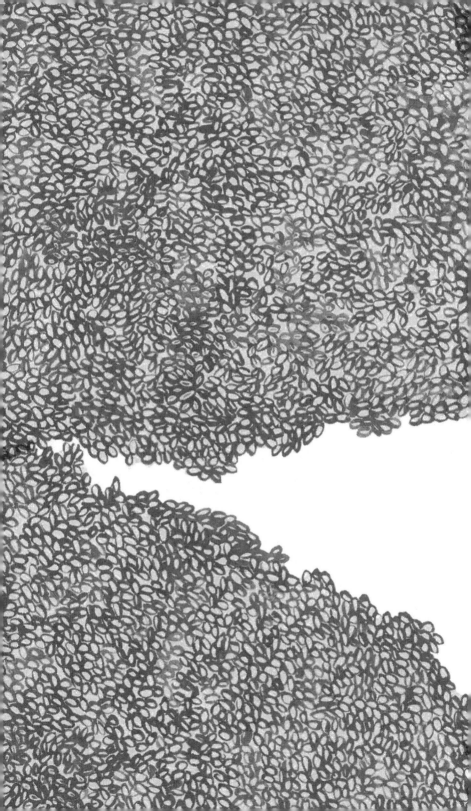

Day 6: Freely He Extends Righteousness (Part Two)

"Now to the one who works, wages are not credited as a gift but as an obligation. However, to the one who does not work but trusts God who justifies the ungodly, their faith is credited as righteousness. David says the same thing when he speaks of the blessedness of the one to whom God credits righteousness apart from works: 'Blessed are those whose transgressions are forgiven, whose sins are covered. Blessed is the one whose sin the Lord will never count against them.'"

— Romans 4:4-8 (NIV) —

FREELY HE EXTENDS RIGHTEOUSNESS

(PART TWO)

There are so many things I want to remember, to learn, and to know. I told someone recently that I am embarrassed to be in my 50's, and yet there are so many things in this world I don't know or have never even heard of. But on the other side, many of them are things I don't want to remember or see. I want someone to see me and not see my messes, my mistakes, my constant striving to be better than I am, or trying to look better, be more talented or funnier. Why am I always striving? Why, as the verse says, am I working for wages? Such as wages of acceptance, having enough, and being liked. These wages are quickly spent. The next fad comes along and everything I had in my bank account is gone.

I am not a perfect person who was saved. I am a sinner who

was spared. My bank account was credited with righteousness. It wasn't a bank error. It was a free gift. I can accept that gift with entitlement, as though it is a debt that was owed to me. Or I can accept this gift with gratitude. I can remember what I deserved, what I have received, and the price that was paid. There is freedom in living in gratitude. I don't care about the balance in my account anymore, because whatever is in there is enough. Our loving Father knows what we need, and he wants to provide.

Father, forgive me every time I get ahead of you and race for what the world has to offer. I know you, I trust you, and I believe in your love for me. Let me live in that love daily.

Dig deeper: Galatians 2:19-21

— *Gena Tarrell, Office Manager*

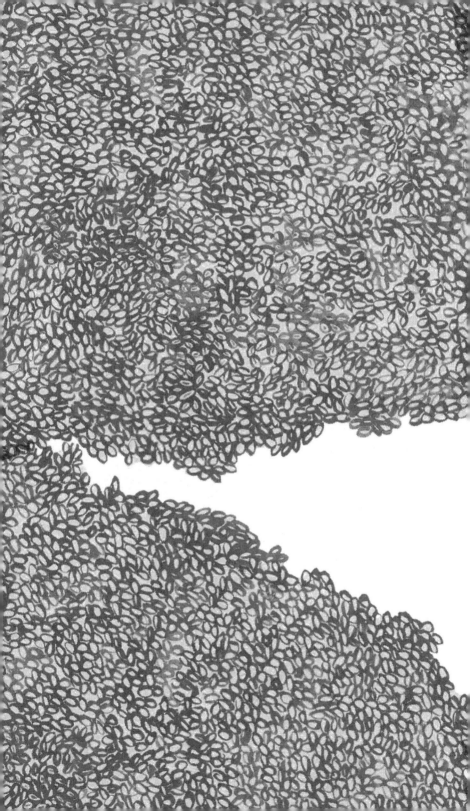

Day 7: Freely He Forgets

"But God found fault with the people and said: 'The days are coming, declares the Lord, when I will make a new covenant with the people of Israel and with the people of Judah. It will not be like the covenant I made with their ancestors when I took them by the hand to lead them out of Egypt, because they did not remain faithful to my covenant, and I turned away from them, declares the Lord. This is the covenant I will establish with the people of Israel after that time, declares the Lord. I will put my laws in their minds and write them on their hearts. I will be their God, and they will be my people. No longer will they teach their neighbor, or say to one another, 'Know the Lord,' because they will all know me, from the least of them to the greatest. For I will forgive their wickedness and will remember their sins no more.' By calling this covenant 'new,' he has made the first one obsolete; and what is obsolete and outdated will soon disappear."

— *Hebrews 8:8-13 (NIV)* —

"The Holy Spirit also testifies to us about this. First he says: 'This is the covenant I will make with them after that time, says the Lord. I will put my laws in their hearts, and I will write them on their minds.' Then he adds: 'Their sins and lawless acts I will remember no more." And where these have been forgiven, sacrifice for sin is no longer necessary."

— Hebrews 10:15-18 (NIV) —

1

FREELY HE FORGETS

The Hebrew people, God's first people, certainly led difficult and burdensome lives under the Law of the Old Covenant. Not only were the Hebrew people responsible for their own actions under His Law, but they also bore the burden of holding their neighbors and children accountable to His Law. What a weight that must have been to bear not only one's own transgressions, but also the transgressions of all those in community with you. If that weren't enough, take a moment to imagine how that responsibility affected the relationships between neighbors, between husband and wife, or between parent and child.

Fortunately, the New Covenant changed everything. No more are we responsible for the teaching of His Law, or the accountability of our neighbors to His Law, as God promises,

"I will put my laws in their minds and write them on their hearts. No longer will they teach their neighbor, or say to one another, 'Know the Lord,' because they will all know me, from the least of them to the greatest." God assumes responsibility to make his Laws known to all people. But more than that, under the New Covenant, not only is this burden of responsibility for others lifted, but the burden of sin is lifted altogether as well.

He forgets our sins. In the selected readings from Hebrews, God promises this to us twice:, *"For I will forgive their wickedness and will remember their sins no more;"* and, *"Their sins and lawless acts I will remember no more."*

God's forgetting is more than just forgiving each of our wrongdoings. God does more than forgive—He forgets. In fact, the cross so completely covered our sins that they no longer exist. He does not look upon our sins, but gazes upon us as His people. Of course this is hard to grasp, perhaps, because such forgetting is beyond human ability and, therefore, a stretch for human understanding.

However, when we can wrap our minds and hearts around God's true disregard for our sins and wicked nature, we can begin to believe that God sees us differently. He sees us wholly and completely. He sees our desire to do right and our desire for His presence in our lives.

In this way, we can change how we see God. Rather than imagining a God who is perpetually frowning in disappointment upon His flawed people, we can see a Father who is gazing lovingly upon His children. When we no longer expect the inevitable judgment that comes from the memory of all our wrongdoing, a weight is lifted.

What does all this mean for us and our relationship with God? God's forgetting allows us to approach Him without fear and/or shame. We can approach God in a way that is conducive to the divine relationship He desires to have with us, which we need and desire to have with Him. The Lord describes this when He says, *"This is the covenant I will establish with the people of Israel after that time, declares the Lord. I will be their God, and they will be my people. For I will forgive their wickedness and will remember their sins no more."*

Dear Lord, help us to accept and hold in our hearts that through the sacrifice made by you and your Son, our sins have truly been forgotten. Give us the courage to approach you with confidence so that we may receive your divine mercy and grace to help us in our time of need. Amen.

— *Lacey A. Leichtnam, Intern 2016-2017*

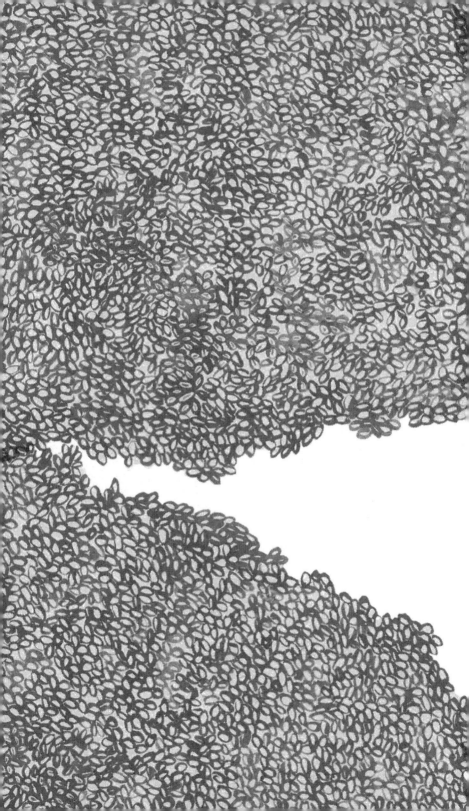

Day 8: Freely He Forgives

"There is no difference between Jew and Gentile, for all have sinned and fall short of the glory of God, and all are justified freely by his grace through the redemption that came by Christ Jesus."
— *Romans 3:22-24 (NIV)* —

FREELY HE FORGIVES

I ran into the grocery store the other day to pick up a few things on my way home from work. When the cashier rang up my purchase, I began digging for my credit card, until I remembered I had left it on the coffee table after making an online purchase the night before. I emptied the cash from my wallet, dug a few coins from some zippered pockets, and I still came up short. Now what? Take everything back and return later? Remove a few items and buy what I can? Ask the clerk to hold everything while I run home and get my card? The guy behind me saw my dilemma. He graciously spotted me a few dollars, insisting that the money was a gift and no debt was owed.

Sometimes we think God's grace works the same way. "Oh, no, there's no way I can pay my debt of sin. But wait, I'll pay what I can, and maybe God will fork over enough to make up the difference. Between the two of us, the bill gets paid."

But that's not the way it works. Here's the reality: We can't even pay a small portion of the bill. Paul says in Romans 3:21-24, *"But now apart from the law the righteousness of God has been made known, to which the Law and Prophets testify. This righteousness is given through faith in Jesus Christ to all who believe. There is no difference between Jew and Gentile, for all have sinned and fall short of the glory of God, and all are justified freely by his grace through the redemption that came by Christ Jesus."*

Paul says the Old Testament law convinces us of sin, and that there is no difference between one type of sinner and another. When he says we fall short, he is not indicating that some fall shorter than others. He means that none of us has anything to contribute.

Ephesians 2:4-5 says it another way: *"But because of his great love for us, God, who is rich in mercy, made us alive with Christ even when we were dead in transgressions—it is by grace you have been saved."* Any and all sin makes us dead. There are not degrees of deadness, with some requiring more to be made alive and others requiring less. God did not simply make up the deficit between what we already have and what we owe. Instead, he paid it all. Here's what this does for me: first, it allows me to rest in the full payment of my debt, knowing that "the incomparable riches of His grace" have paid the full price. Secondly, it keeps me from counting morality as pocket change which I can contribute to the purchase of salvation. It prohibits a false accounting system of debits and credits that has me owing less than the guy next to me. The One who is rich in mercy paid my entire bill—and yours—freely by His grace through Jesus Christ.

Dear Father, thank you for paying my entire bill. Remind me that my moral pocket change does not help with the cost. Please help me not to judge other people, but to treat them with the grace and mercy that you have given me. Amen.

Dig deeper: Romans 3:19-24 and Ephesians 2:1-10

— *Susan Terveen, Clinical Therapist, Stronghold Spearfish*

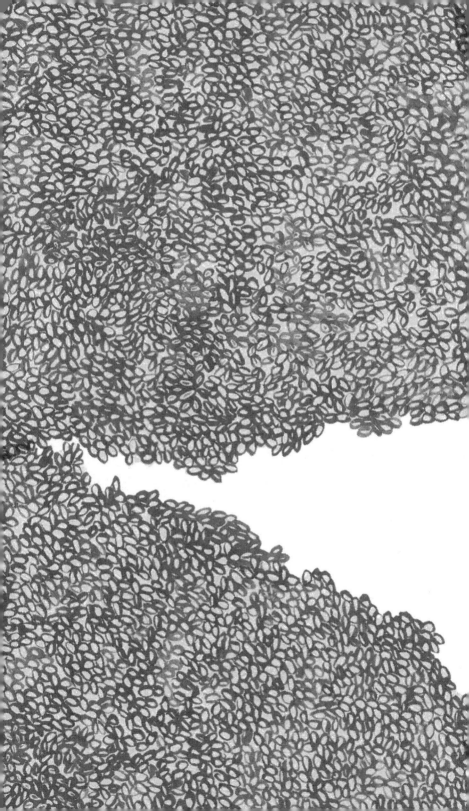

Day 9: Freely He Grants Peace (Part One)

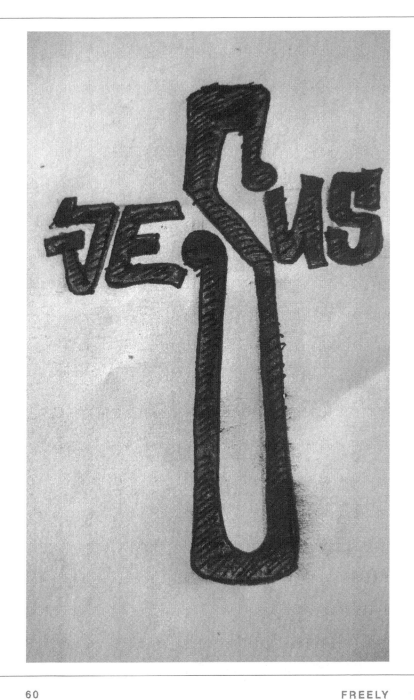

"Peace I leave with you; my peace I give you. I do not give to you as the world gives. Do not let your hearts be troubled and do not be afraid."

— John 14:27 (NIV) —

9

FREELY HE GRANTS PEACE

(PART ONE)

I remember one time driving home with my mom on a road trip. I was about 8 years old, and the fog was thick. It was so thick that it seemed like we were the only vehicle on the road, and we had to drive very slowly. I remember feeling afraid. Before I shut my eyes to go to sleep, I noticed the bright yellow lines on the road that showed us which way to go. When I awoke we were safely home.

Life can get so "foggy" sometimes with the external and internal things we may deal with on a daily basis. We have this great promise from God through Jesus Christ His son, that though we may feel troubled, alone, and lost at times, He promises to be near us. He freely gives us peace. His peace empowers us to walk strongly throughout our daily lives. He promises to give us peace in the midst of it all, which is our inheritance as His beloved children.

Lord Jesus, I thank you for being near to me today, as I go through life's challenges. I thank you for filling me with your peace and walking with me today. Let your peace dispel any fear I am feeling today, allowing me to be victorious. In Jesus' name, amen.

— *Joshua Duncan, Intern 2015-2016*

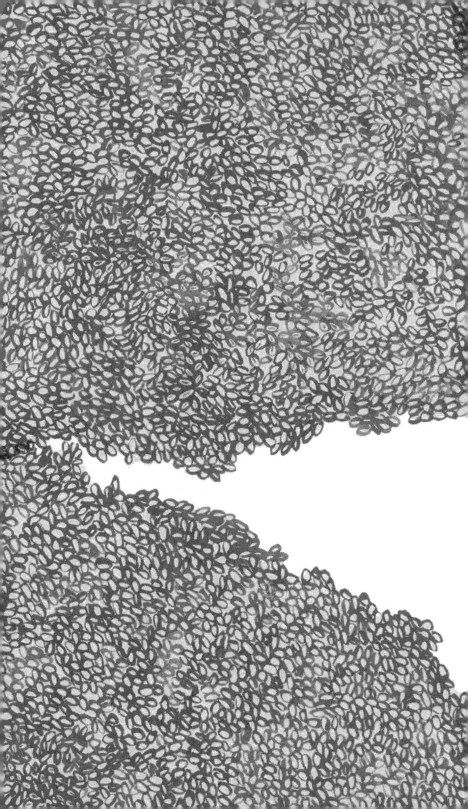

Day 10: Freely He Grants Peace (Part Two)

"Peace I leave with you; my peace I give you. I do not give to you as the world gives. Do not let your hearts be troubled and do not be afraid."

— John 14:27 (NIV) —

FREELY HE GRANTS PEACE

(PART TWO)

How many times have I felt afraid or experienced a lack of peace? Sending my kids out the door to kindergarten or college, watching them back out of the driveway for their first solo driving experience, buckling my seatbelt before takeoff on an airplane, wondering how to repair a strained relationship, losing a loved one; those are all troubling moments when my heart doesn't feel settled. And while there is usually another emotion connected to the turbulent feeling in my heart—either joy, fear, pain, or sadness — the unsettled core of it goes against the faith Jesus asks me to put in Him. Jesus' peace extends beyond the circumstances we face in this life. The peace He provides is steady and unshakeable.

His peace is a gift, a promise He made to His disciples as

He prepared to leave them on this earth. He promised to send the Holy Spirit in His place. That promise extends to all of us. We have the gift of calling on the Holy Spirit whenever we need to.

Dear Jesus, thank you for the peace you put into my heart and for the gift of the Holy Spirit. When I am afraid and full of worry, give me the courage to hand my fears over to you. Awaken in me the unshakeable faith to trust the peace and goodness you have provided for me and my loved ones, until we join you in Heaven.

— *Jodi Merritt, Clinical Therapist*

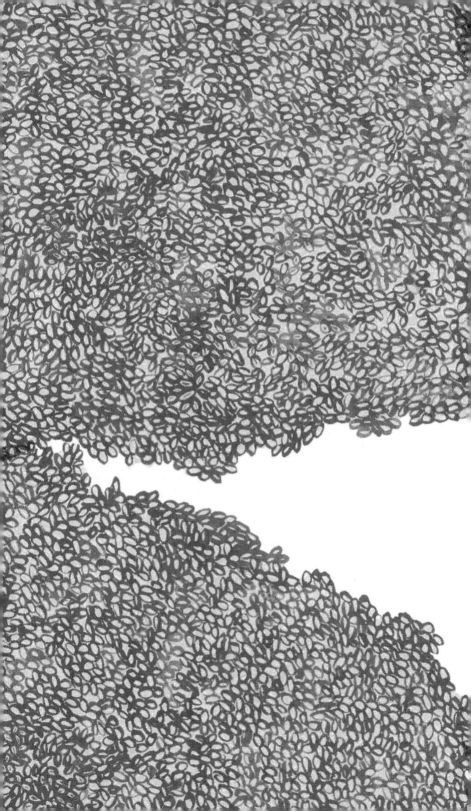

Day 11: Freely He Will Return (Part One)

"Brothers and sisters, we do not want you to be uninformed about those who sleep in death, so that you do not grieve like the rest of mankind, who have no hope."

— 1 Thessalonians 4:13 (NIV) —

"Everyone has to die once, then face the consequences. Christ's death was also a one-time event, but it was a sacrifice that took care of sins forever. And so, when he next appears, the outcome for those eager to meet him is, precisely, salvation."

— Hebrews 9:27-28 (MSG) —

DAY
11

FREELY HE WILL RETURN

(PART ONE)

Freely (no barriers, able to move forward) He will *return* (go back). Those are words that don't seem to fit in the same sentence. When you are finally free of the very place where you were enslaved (a toxic work environment, a career path, a dysfunctional family, an abusive marriage, an addiction, war, gossip, fame, etc.) you don't go back to it!

Our Father saw our condition, and He had empathy for us and our tendency to choose things that can hurt us. He sent His Son back to the streets to save as many as He could through the cross, and for others He left a road map (His Word). As Christians, death is a transition; it's temporary; it's sadness; it's emptiness and it's devastation. But it's sprinkled with the hope we have as believers, so that we are not left in that sad, empty place.

Father, help us find hope and courage as we move out of the places in our lives where we are not free. Thank you for seeing us and sympathizing with us.

— *Lorri Chambers*

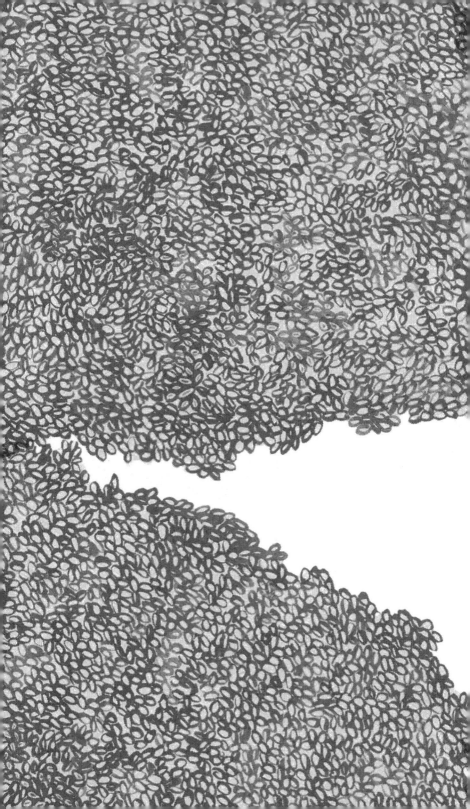

Day 12: Freely He Will Return (Part Two)

FREELY HE WILL RETURN

(PART TWO)

To freely return, one has to have been there in the first place and want to come back. Being a Canadian and living in the States, my thoughts often return to my home country. My happy place is Lake Louise, Alberta with the beauty of the Rockies, a crystal clear glacial lake, and the smell of pine. And although I enjoy the scenery and the different terrain of my home province, it is not what draws me home. It is my family and friends—relationships.

There are people that I have a special relationship with. They're on a must-see-list when I go home. I look forward to the laughs, sharing memories of when we did this or that, the heartfelt talks, knowing I belong and fit in, and picking up right where we left off, as though I never left. There is a longing and desire for something you are passionate for, for something you miss and must go back to, such as relationships!

Freely implies a choice, not out of obligation, but out of a heart of love. Jesus came the first time in order to bear our sin. When He comes the second time it will be *"to bring salvation to those who are waiting for him,"* Hebrews 8:28.

Christ freely gives us the future of being with Him again. He will return, and *"The dead in Christ will rise first. After that, we who are still alive and are left will be caught up together with them in the clouds to meet the Lord in the air,"* 1 Thessalonians 4:16-17.

Death is not the end of the story. The story continues with the victorious return of the King of kings, the Lord of lords. *"Therefore encourage one another with these words,"* 1 Thessalonians 4:18. Come, oh, Lord Jesus, come!

Father, you have called us sons and daughters. That makes us your family. And as Jesus wept at the grave of Lazarus, you join us as we mourn the loss of our loved ones. Yet our hope is in Jesus and His triumphant return, and, therefore, we will not lose heart. Strengthen us and sustain us until that day. Amen.

Dig deeper: Hebrews 9:27-28 and 1 Thessalonians 4:13-18

— *Earl Witt, Clinical Therapist*

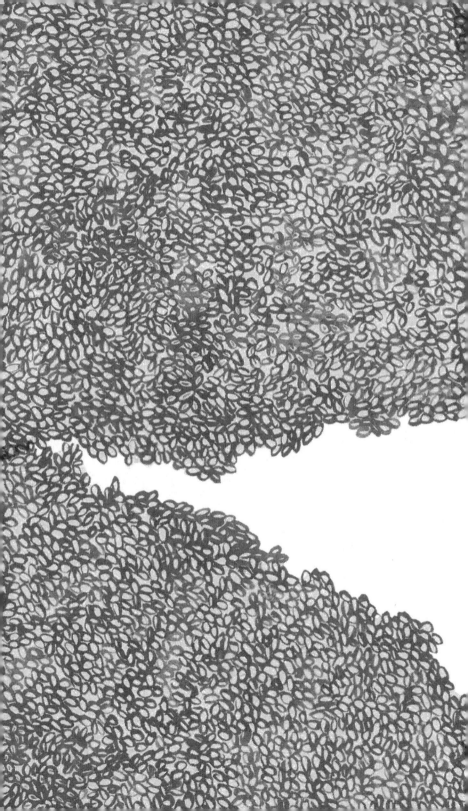

Day 13: Freely He Will Return (Part Three)

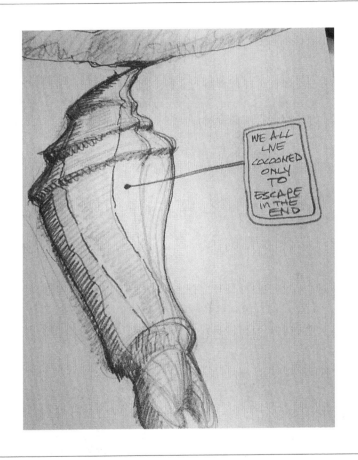

"And now, dear brothers and sisters, we want you to know what will happen to the believers who have died so you will not grieve like people who have no hope."

— *1 Thessalonians 4:13 (NLT)* —

13

FREELY HE WILL RETURN

(PART THREE)

July 8, 2018

My oldest daughter and I stepped off the Royal Caribbean Liberty of the Seas in Galveston from what we called our "Epic Trip, 2018 Edition." We were in the tradition of taking a big trip together every summer and this was our 6th year in a row, and the first time we had cruised in addition to the 17-hour drive from South Dakota. We had a great time, but I was anxious to get back home to see my husband, and especially my nearly 6-month-old grandson, who we would see on our way back.

As is our custom, I did much of the driving while my daughter navigated us through unfamiliar cities and traffic. An hour into the drive, we both commented on unusual incom-

ing phone and Facebook calls, which we dismissed as "odd."
When my daughter finally answered one she recognized, from
one of her sisters, time stood still and I was catapulted into an
unknown world of shock, disaster, and grief. My husband of
34 years was gone. Gone, as in dead, leaving me that terrible
"W" word at age 54, my three daughters fatherless, and my
grandson, Papa-less. As shock gave way to waves of unbearable
pain, I was startled by what clearly came to mind and would be
repeated over and over again, almost as a mantra, in the chaotic
and stressful days and weeks to come: "He's in heaven. He is in
heaven. My beloved is right now, in this very moment, in the
presence of Jesus!" It was a focus and a way to take the next
breath.

I remember very little of that day, but I know I spent most
of it gripping the wheel of my daughter's Hyundai so tightly
my hands grew numb. Driving kept me from completely falling
apart. I spent hours on the phone trying to piece together what
had happened and clutching my daughter's hand in desperation
for the comfort of connection, as we endured the endless trip
home together.

While some details of that horrible day have gone cloudy, I
do remember my mantra, and I cling to it still. "He-is-in-heav-
en." Lamentations 3:22 says, *"Because of the Lord's great love we
are not consumed."* My daughters and I still grieve deeply. Many
others grieve with us, as my husband touched so many lives with
his. We are broken and struggling and wracked with inevitable

regrets and sadness. But we are not consumed by our grief. 1 Thessalonians 4:13 proclaims that we ought not grieve as people who have no hope. Our primary goal as we celebrated his life was to give people hope in the midst of their sorrow. I stand firm in the hope that I will see my beloved when I join him in heaven, or when Jesus freely returns with a commanding shout, with the call of the archangel, and with the trumpet call of God. Until that day, I cling to hope.

Father, right here in the pain of our deepest sorrow and brokenness, you are with us. You, too, knew deep grief, and you sympathize with us. You offer us hope with the promise of eternity with you, our healer, our comforter, our God.

— *Lorri Chambers*

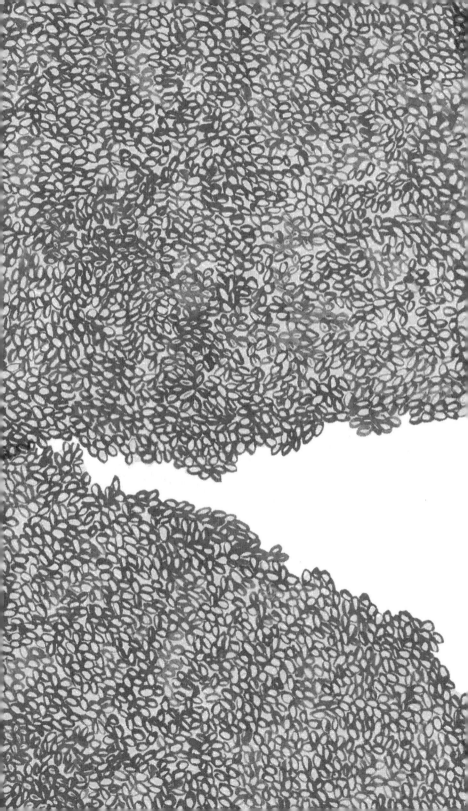

Day 14: Freely He Gives Grace

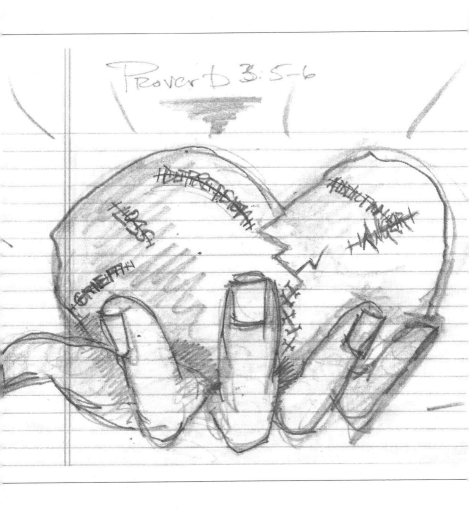

"But to each one of us grace was given according to the measure of Christ's gift."

— *Ephesians 4:7 (NKJV)* —

Author Timothy Paul Jones tells the story of taking his adopted daughter to Disney World: "Our middle daughter had been previously adopted by another family, but they never quite integrated the adopted child into their family of biological children. After a couple of rough years, they dissolved the adoption. We ended up welcoming an eight-year-old girl into our home.

For one reason or another, whenever our daughter's previous family vacationed at Disney World, they took their biological children with them, but they left their adopted daughter with a family friend. Usually—at least in the child's mind—this happened because she did something wrong.

Once I found out about this history, I made plans to take her to Disney World. In the month leading up to our trip to the

Magic Kingdom, she stole food and she whispered insults that were carefully crafted to hurt her older sister. As the days on the calendar moved closer to the trip, her mutinies multiplied.

A couple of days before our family headed to Florida, I pulled our daughter into my lap to talk through her latest escapade. 'I know what you're going to do,' she stated flatly. 'You're not going to take me to Disney World, are you?' By God's grace, I asked her, 'Is this trip something we're doing as a family?' She nodded with her brown eyes wide and tear-rimmed. 'Are you part of this family?' She nodded again. 'Then you're going with us. Sure, there may be some consequences to help you remember what's right and what's wrong, but you're part of our family, and we're not leaving you behind.'"

After our first day, she was exhausted, pensive, and a little weepy at times, but her month-long facade of rebellion had faded. When bedtime rolled around, I prayed with her, held her, and asked, 'So how was your first day at Disney World? She closed her eyes and snuggled down into her stuffed unicorn. After a few moments, she opened her eyes ever so slightly. 'Daddy,' she said, 'I finally got to go to Disney World. But it wasn't because I was good; it's because I'm yours.'"

We are welcomed into the family of God when we accept Christ as our Savior. However, it is not because we deserve it, we've earned it, or we've done everything right. It's because of God's grace. The definition of grace is unmerited favor.

Even when we make a mistake or make bad choices and Satan says God has given up on us, we need to remember what *Paul said: "We are more than conquerors through Him ...who loved us,"* Romans 8:37 (NKJV).

As Julia H. Johnston penned in a beautiful hymn:

"Marvelous grace of our loving Lord,

Grace that exceeds our sin and our guilt!

Yonder on Calvary's mount outpoured,

There where the blood of the Lamb was spilt.

Grace, grace, God's grace,

Grace that will pardon and cleanse within;

Grace, grace, God's grace,

Grace that is greater than all our sin!"

Lord, today I live in your family not because I'm good, but because I'm yours! Help me to apply and live in your grace every day.

— *Larry Reed, Former Clinical Therapist*

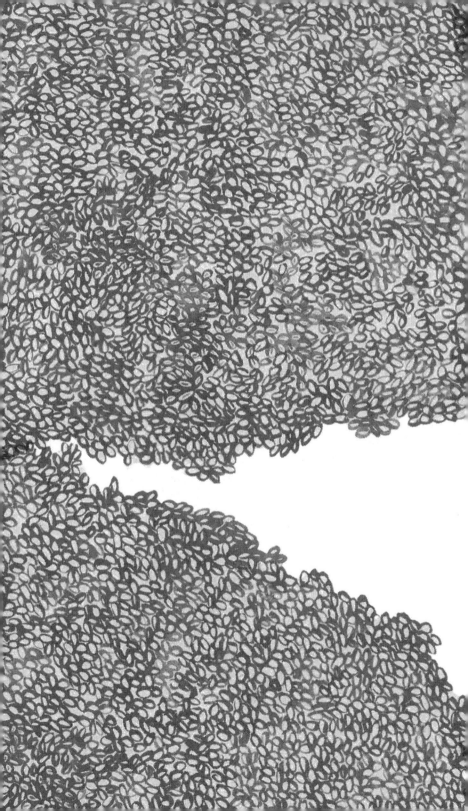

Day 15: Freely He Likes You

FREELY

"The Lord your God is with you, the Mighty Warrior who saves. He will take great delight in you; in his love he will no longer rebuke you, but will rejoice over you with singing."

— *Zephaniah 3:17 (NIV)* —

15

FREELY HE LIKES YOU

Excerpts from JC's video with Clear Frame Media:

"Real fellowship is uncomfortable to people. We hide behind glasses and costumes. We are afraid (and often it is true) that others will get freaked out when we take our dress clothes off. People have to learn the comfort of authenticity. I ask people in my office, "If Jesus walked in the door what would He say to you right now?" People look at my door and turn away from it.

I ask, "What does that mean?" They say, "It aint good." They ask me what I think He would say.

I say, "He would come to the door and say, 'hey, I am so glad to see you. Can I sit down next to you?'" Then He would put His arm around you and ask, "how you been? What's up? I can tell you ain't been doin' good." When I give this scenario, people start crying. I am shocked. This is the gospel! How come it's a surprise? People wonder about a God like that, but that is the only dude I know. The other guys I have in my head, I kick them out. They bang on the door, but I am working hard to not listen.

When I share the God I know, people then open up. I tell them, "He is excited to walk in the door and meet with you. He likes you." Most are surprised when I say God likes you just as you are now, with your addiction or whatever you are bringing to the table. Those things don't disqualify you. He wants you to change, but He is not disgusted or appalled by your behavior. The therapist is not appalled. The therapist likes you. People are shocked by grace.

My identity has been changed from sinner to saint. I want people to experience a relationship with someone who honors them, whether they are a Christian or not. They are the King's child. I have to treat them like royalty.

When you come to Stronghold, you meet with someone who is broken, too. They can walk with you and aren't afraid to speak truth with you. We are grounded in God's principles, but we are not evangelizers."

Father, may those who read this know you like them! You rejoice over them with singing. They are your children! Help us, as your servants, to treat all those who cross our paths as your precious child. In your loving name we pray. Amen.

— *Dr. JC Chambers, Co-founder (1959-2018)*

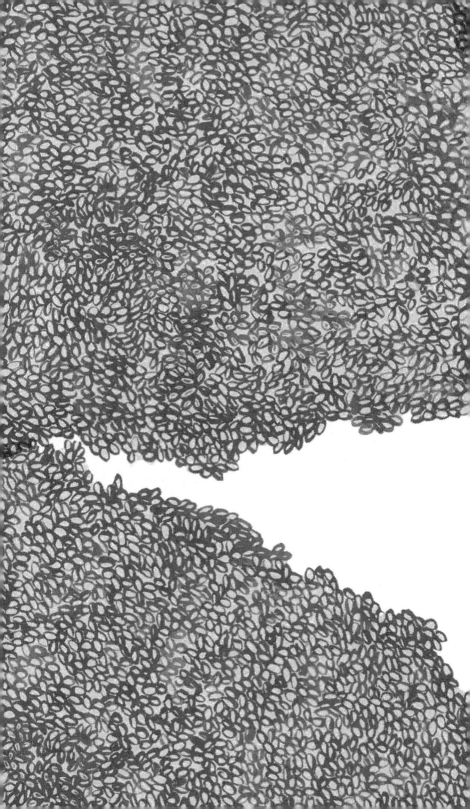

Day 16: Freely He Loves

God IS Love

"Now that I, your Lord and Teacher, have washed your feet, also wash one another's feet. I have set you an example that you should do as I have done for you."

— *John 13:14-15 (NIV)* —

GOD IS LOVE

Is love a verb or a noun? Is it a feeling, or is it something we do? God demonstrates His love for us through action, because He knows it is through experience that we feel.

In a 2013 Huffington Post article titled "The Man Who Used His Own Body As A Crash Pad," Elizabeth Svoboda writes about love in action. She describes how veteran Texan skydiving instructor, Dave Hartsock, made a life-giving decision seconds before impact while doing a tandem jump where both chutes failed. The hero opted to use control toggles to rotate his body so that he'd cushion Shirley Dygert, a grandmother and first-time diver. Hartsock took the brunt of the impact, saving Dygert's life. Her injuries were not life-threatening, but Hartsock paid a monumental price. The fall paralyzed him from the neck down. Dygert reports she sometimes tears up when she thinks about what a sacrifice her instructor made for her, saying, "How can somebody have that much love for another person?"

If this is how much love one human can have for another, how much greater is our Father's love for us?

God is our instructor. He sent His Son to be fully human so that He could understand what it is like to hurt, to be afraid, to be frustrated, and to feel joy. He knows firsthand what physical and emotional pain feels like. Why would He do that? Because He loves us freely. He didn't have to, but He chose to.

When Jesus died on the cross, He freely gave love. Many times people think God punished His Son on the cross. But does that match a loving God? No, He did not punish His Son. Jesus freely gave His life to us, while we were still sinners. It's a free gift. We don't have to do anything to earn it.

A famous verse about love is *John 3:16: "For God so loved the world, that he gave His one and only Son, that whoever believes in Him shall not perish but have eternal life."* Further, the author states in verse 17, *"For God did not send His Son into the world to condemn the world, but to save the world, through Him."*

So, you mean when I hear that shaming voice in my head (you know the one), that's not God? He's not saying, "I can't believe you. You'll never get it right." No, God did not come in human form to condemn the world. Rather, He is saying, "I don't condemn you. I understand you. Come to me and learn more about my love."

Want to learn more? He's got some pretty cool things to say. Dig into John 3:13-21 and John 13:1-17. Feel the love. It's free.

Dear Heavenly Father, we are grateful that we know love because we first received love. It is good to know you are love. Freely, you give this love to us. What a relief to know we can't earn it. You just give it to us. And we can't undo this, we can't mess this up. We don't know love like this in human form. We say we love our family and friends unconditionally, but we have our biases, no matter how hard we try not to. It is good to know you have no biases, and that your love is for all of us. Thank you for your love and all the ways we experience it. Amen.

— *Andrea Bloch, Intern 2013-14*

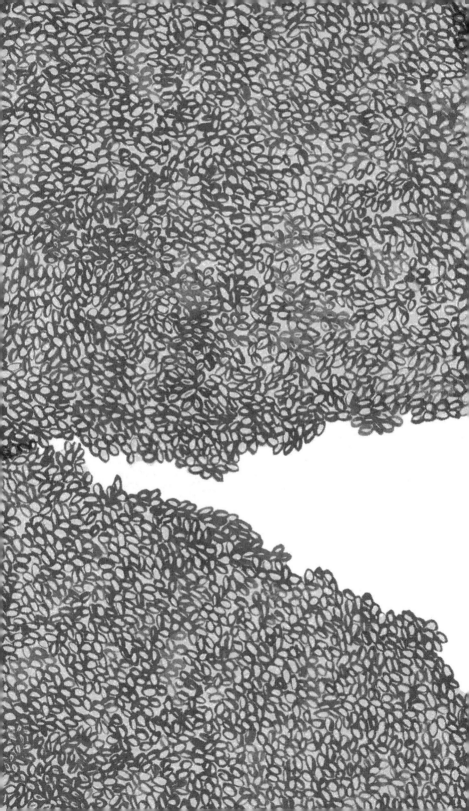

Day 17: Freely He Promises Life

"Anyone who meets a testing challenge head-on and manages to stick it out is mighty fortunate. For such persons loyally in love with God, the reward is life and more life."

— *James 1:12 (MSG)* —

"Blessed is the one who perseveres under trial because, having stood the test, that person will receive the crown of life that the Lord has promised to those who love him."

— *James 1:12 (NIV)* —

FREELY HE PROMISES LIFE

My dad is, not was, is, the best coach I know. And I've had a lot of coaches over the years.

I started playing basketball in the 4th grade. The Jefferson Shooters was our team name. Shooters we were, but point scorers we most certainly were not. The coach? My dad, of course. I absolutely loved being coached by him. So did the rest of my team. I took great pride in being the coach's daughter. As 4th graders, I'll be honest, we were terrible. As 5th graders, we were only a few steps up from that.

It wasn't until 7th and 8th grade that my team, Edison Liberty, actually manifested into something great and we were able to compete with other teams. We were able to shoot and actually score and finally win. I can speed up the story of years of transformation with my team in a few sentences, but it did, in fact, take that much time—years. As we entered middle school, I remember telling my dad, "Dad, if you yell at me, I will not listen to you." Friends, he never yelled at me or my teammates. To clarify, yelling for no reason was what I meant when I gave him that ultimatum. He didn't yell, but he had many reasons he could have from 4th to 8th grade.

What I remember most about my dad is that despite every challenge faced, every loss, every knuckle-headed kid that joined our team, every frustration, turnover, or bad out-of-bounds play, he never abandoned us or stopped coaching. And when he saw we were frustrated or feeling like we let him down, he always made it a point at the end of the game to tell us that he was proud of us for doing our best, for sticking it out, for not giving up.

You see, it was never about the wins or losses when my dad coached. He was competitive, don't get me wrong, but he wanted to teach. That's who he was, a teacher in the form of a coach. My dad faced many trials in his short 57 years, and each time he'd find a way, just like he found a way to coach us through to the end. With each trial, he came out on the other side having learned something.

God didn't promise life would be easy, and it's a myth that God never gives us more than we can handle. But He did promise that if we persevere, keep going, and hold strong, our reward is life and more life. In Deuteronomy 31:6 we are told, *"Be strong and courageous. Do not be afraid or terrified because of them, for the Lord your God goes with you; He will never leave you nor forsake you."*

I am confident in knowing that my dad is in Heaven, and he's probably playing basketball with God as we speak. My dad stood the test, knowing that he was never left nor forgotten. I, too, cling to this promise, that as I stand here in the valley of the darkest season of my life, one day I will have life and more life because I kept going.

Hey God, we are so thankful for your promise that even in our darkest moments, if we keep going, we will receive life in you. Help us to remember that even when we feel we can't keep moving, you remain with us. Your promise is so, so good. Amen.

— *Alyssa Chambers*

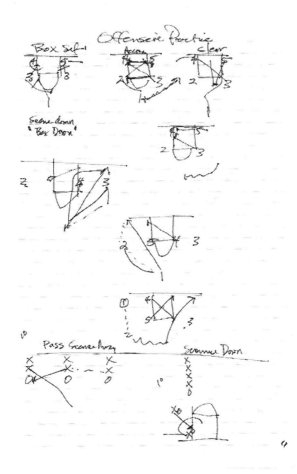

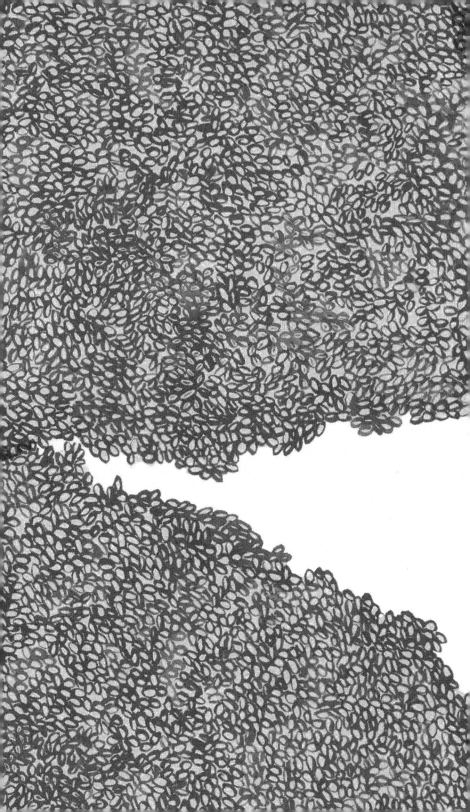

Day 18: Freely He Promises Gentleness (Part One)

"Come to me, all you who are weary and burdened, and I will give you rest. Take my yoke upon you and learn from me, for I am gentle and humble in heart, and you will find rest for your souls. For my yoke is easy and my burden is light."

— *Matthew 11:28-30 (NIV)* —

"Cast all your anxiety on him because he cares for you."

— 1 Peter 5:7 (NIV) —

(PART ONE)

Imagine that the weight of life's struggles you are under can be lifted. Worry, fear, anxiety, depression, hurt—you don't have to carry it anymore! Someone else has cut the burden away and taken it for you.

In the movie *The Mission,* Mendoza (Robert De Niro), a slave trader in the 1740s, is trying to do penance for kidnapping and selling natives to plantation owners, and killing his half-brother in a duel. He joins a group of Jesuit Priests to reach Guarani natives in Argentina. Mendoza accompanies the Jesuits on their return journey, dragging a heavy bundle containing his armor and sword up cliffs. Dragging it behind him, he almost falls many times because it is so heavy. The journey is hard, and he is exhausted by the weight of the baggage, but he can't let it go. As they reach the top of the cliff in the natives' territory tension built. The Guarani recognized him and who he was, but they saw the burden he was dragging and cut it loose. Mendoza began to cry and the people embraced him. His heavy load was gone, and he received love and forgiveness.

The burdens we carry can be so heavy and more than we can bear. Jesus wants to carry them for us if we'll let him. He promises rest, and He is gentle. His yoke is easy, and His burden is light. We just have to be willing to give it up and ask Him to take it. It sounds easy, but it's not always so. Fear of not being in control, fear of the unknown, not being able to trust—these get in the way. But when we discover that God is gentle, loving, trustworthy, and waiting with open arms to take it from us, then we surrender it to Him and find peace. The struggle is gone.

Jesus wants us to come to Him. He invites us. Will you accept His invitation and experience the rest He offers?

Father, help us come to know the relief that comes from laying down our burdens at your feet. You offer to carry them so we don't have to. All we have to do is let go.

— *Grace Lee, Former Support Staff*

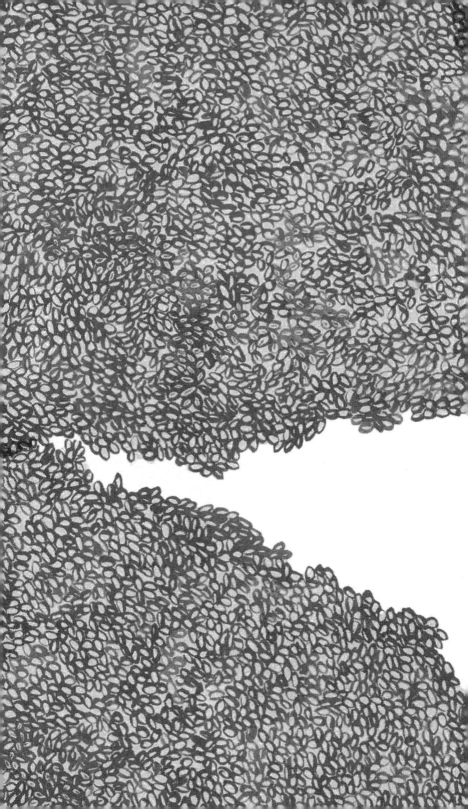

Day 19: Freely He Promises Gentleness (Part Two)

FREELY

"God means what he says. What he says goes. His powerful Word is sharp as a surgeon's scalpel, cutting through everything, whether doubt or defense, laying us open to listen and obey. Nothing and no one is impervious to God's Word. We can't get away from it—no matter what. Now that we know what we have—Jesus, this great High Priest with ready access to God—let's not let it slip through our fingers. We don't have a priest who is out of touch with our reality. He's been through weakness and testing, experienced it all—all but the sin. So let's walk right up to him and get what he is so ready to give. Take the mercy, accept the help."

— Hebrews 4:12-16 (MSG) —

My granddaughter, Aubrie, loves candy. She loves candy so much that when we vacation together and each person gets to pick a spot or activity, Aubrie chooses a candy store. My daughter, Jenni, on the other hand, loves feeding her children healthy food. Hence, there is tension and, at times, hiding. One Christmas, Aubrie was given a play tent in which she spent most of Christmas afternoon. When it was time to pick up and put things away for the day, we found many, many candy wrappers in the tent.

Just as the candy escapade was not hidden from Aubrie's mother, so our actions are visible to our Father. Just as being found out made my tender-hearted granddaughter cry (without a word being spoken by her mother), so we tend to cringe with fear, guilt, shame, or some other painful emotion.

Aubrie didn't know her mother had the same inclination to overindulge in candy as a little girl. Her mother remembered and understood that temptation and dealt gently with her beloved daughter. Jesus is also "in touch with our reality." As the verse says above, *"God means what He says."* Don't forget what He says: "I love you, I died for you, I am always with you, you have a home with Me, you are redeemed, I know you." Let those gentle words encourage us to respond in obedience, without fear, guilt, or shame.

Lord, so often the words I focus on are not your words of love, caring, and acceptance. Help me understand I am known and loved by you. Help that love manifest itself through me to reach others in your love. Let me be like the beggar who has found bread and can't wait to tell the rest of the beggars. Amen.

— *Gena Tarrell, Office Manager*

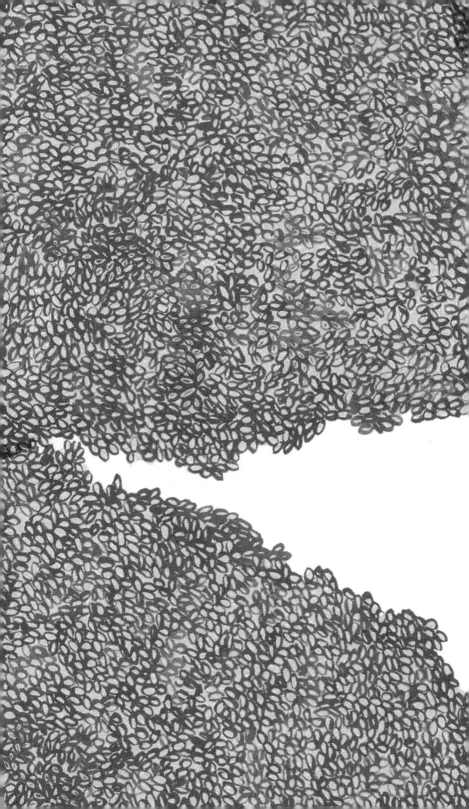

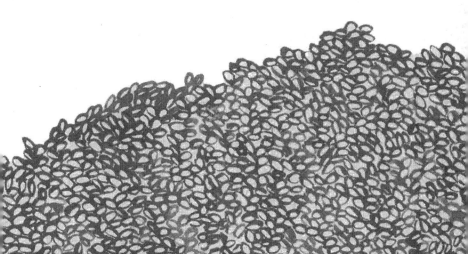

Day 20: Freely He Reconciles

FREELY

Therefore, just as sin entered the world through one man, and death through sin, and in this way death came to all people, because all sinned."

— Romans 5:12 (NIV) —

"...for all have sinned and fall short of the glory of God."

— Romans 3:23 (NIV) —

FREELY HE RECONCILES

Reconcile is not a word that is common in our vocabulary. The origin of this word means "to make good again or repair." The word "again" implies that there was a state prior to something happening. Adam and Eve were the only people that experienced being sinless/good. As Paul said in 2 Corinthians 5:12, "In Christ" means we are a "new creation." To be in Christ means to have security, acceptance, future assurance of eternal life, and participation with Christ. *"All of this is from God, who [freely] reconciled us to Himself through Christ,"* and, *"...gave us the ministry of reconciliation,"* 1 Corinthians 5:18 (NIV).

This is the foundational piece of Stronghold Counseling Services. We have the privilege to participate with Jesus in the tearing down of strongholds in lives (beliefs contrary to the word of God), as well as giving a stronghold (sanctuary) to where one can come and find rest. We cannot give what we do not have; but what we do have, we have the opportunity to give to those who come our way.

In one word, grace! To experience grace is to be given something that is not earned, merited, or deserved. On the contrary, we deserve the consequences of our sinful behaviors; however, we have been freely given Jesus, and we have been freely reconciled and "made good again—repaired." This can only happen and be experienced in relationships; no one can do this on their own.

Father, thank you that you finish what you start. You leave nothing undone as you continue the work and you allow us to work alongside you in the restoration of those you died for: everyone Give us the words to speak of the work you have done in us, so that "whoever believes in Him should not perish, but have eternal life. Amen.

Dig deeper: 2 Corinthians 5:17-21 and Colossians 1:19-23

— *Earl Witt, Clinical Therapist*

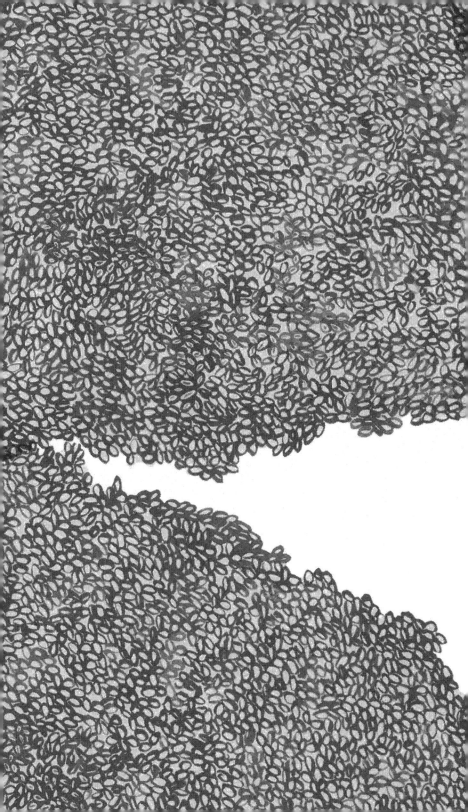

Day 21: Freely He Redeems

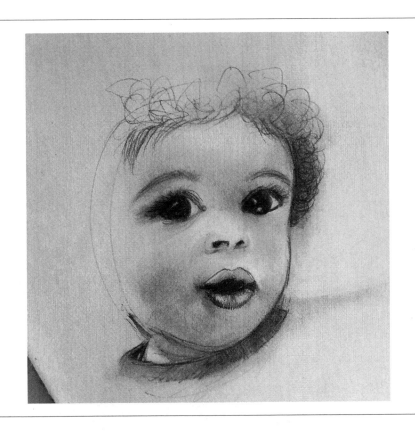

FREELY

"But when the time had fully come, God sent forth his Son, born of woman, born under the law, to redeem those who were under the law, so that we might receive adoption as sons."

— Galations 4:4-5 (RSV) —

21

FREELY HE REDEEMS

Anyone else get impatient? As in (insert your context: grocery store line, traffic light, unending work tasks, stubborn face of a toddler/teenager/aging parent, you get the picture), "hey, girl, hey, get out of my way. I'm ready to move, now!" I wish this wasn't me, but it is.

Patience definitely does not come easily for me. I see an opportunity and want it to come about ASAP. I see the way things "should be" and am ready for them to be that way five minutes ago. But something I've noticed about the way of Jesus is that it's not microwaveable. Jesus talks about transformation and redemption in His kingdom in agricultural terms: a seed scattered on the ground, planted in the soil, growing in the darkness, being harvested at just the right time. C'mon Jesus. Couldn't you give us something like the Kingdom of God is like a chia seed pet, blossoming seemingly overnight (or, as the packaging says, in approximately 4-7 days)?

Nope, God's way is patient. His ways are not our ways. They are slow and steady, consistent and wild.

The Galatians verses in today's devotional scripture reading do tell us that His work is finished. Through Christ, we are included and chosen, and we have redemption, forgiveness, and the Holy Spirit. These are present tenses and realities in light of the work of Jesus. Ephesians 1:13 tells us, *"You also were included in Christ when you heard the word of truth...having believed you were marked in Him."* In and through Christ, the work of God is already finished.

And yet, it's also not. The life of the Kingdom of God and the invitation of Jesus to His ways are, to return to the agricultural terms, blossoming, growing, and not yet here in the fullness of fruits. Don't we see that reality in our day to day lives? Don't we see the reality of the already finished work and not yet completed work of redemption? Do we see in regular life events, like in the beauty of a family joining together after fighting or discord to wrestle with how to manage forgiveness and change? Do we see it in the peace we experience despite ongoing stress and tension in our work or parenting roles? Do we see it in the way in which our physical or emotional limitations lead us to turn to others for support and help? Beauty and pain is commingled. Redemption is here and also not yet complete.

Jesus, this message is hard for me sometimes. I wish your redemption was already fully complete here and now. I long for that day and pray for that day. I trust in the coming of that day, the day in which we will receive full rights of being your children. Because I am your child, I am no longer a slave, but a child of God; and since I am a child of God, I trust that you also have made me an heir—your heir (Galatians 4:5-7). I am an heir to the fullness of your redemption in the coming Kingdom. I trust in the already and the not yet, that as children of faith we are growing in trust, being strengthened as we wait, developing patience and learning to demonstrate your grace in the here and now. Your redemption is here and it is coming in its fullness. Amen.

— *Mikaela Campbell, Intern 2011-2012*

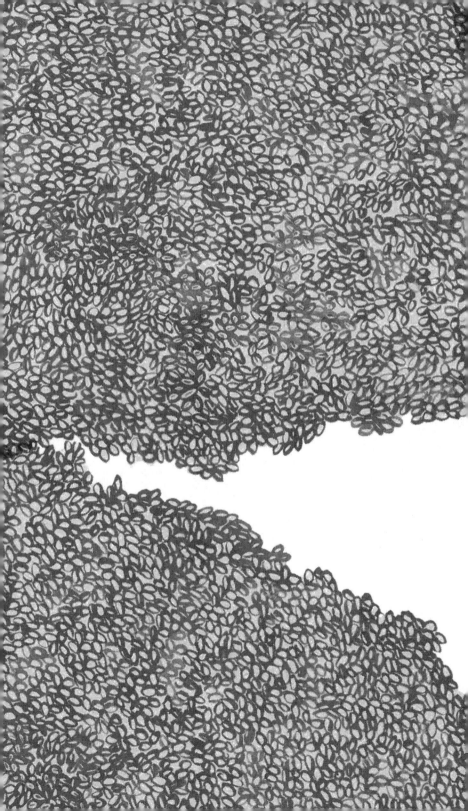

Day 22: Freely He Relinquished Judgement (Part One)

"Therefore, there is no longer any condemnation awaiting those who are in union with the Messiah Yeshua. Why? Because the Torah of the Spirit, which produces this life in union with Messiah Yeshua, has set me free from the 'Torah' of sin and death. For what the Torah could not do by itself, because it lacked the power to make the old nature cooperate, God did by sending his own Son as a human being with a nature like our own sinful one [but without sin]. God did this in order to deal with sin, and in so doing he executed the punishment against sin in human nature, so that the just requirement of the Torah might be fulfilled in us who do not run our lives according to what our old nature wants but according to what the Spirit wants."

— *Romans 8:1-4 (CJB)* —

"You were dead because of your sins, that is, because of your 'foreskin,' your old nature. But God made you alive along with the Messiah by forgiving you all your sins. He wiped away the bill of charges against us. Because of the regulations, it stood as a testimony against us; but he removed it by nailing it to the execution-stake. Stripping the rulers and authorities of their power, he made a public spectacle of them, triumphing over them by means of the stake. So don't let anyone pass judgement on you in connection with eating and drinking, or in regard to a Jewish festival or Rosh-Hodesh or Shabbat. These are a shadow of things that are coming, but the body is of the Messiah. Don't let anyone deny you the prize by insisting that you engage in self-mortification or angel-worship. Such people are always going on about some vision they have had, and they vainly puff themselves up by their worldly outlook. They fail to hold to the Head, from whom the whole body, receiving supply and being held together by its joints and ligaments, grows as God makes it grow. If, along with the Messiah, you died to the elemental spirits of the world, then why, as if you still belonged to the world, are you letting yourselves be bothered by its rules? 'Don't touch this!' 'Don't eat that!' 'Don't handle the other!' Such prohibitions are concerned with things meant to perish by being used [not by being avoided!], and they are based on man-made rules and teachings. They do indeed have the outward appearance of wisdom, with their self-imposed religious observances, false humility and asceticism; but they have no value at all in restraining people from indulging their old nature."

— *Colossians 2:13-23 (CJB)* —

(PART ONE)

The simple truth is that God relinquished judgement upon us, the unjust. The Messiah Yeshua destroyed the accuser's truthful sins recorded against us by obliterating the document [the Law] by means of the execution stake. The physical symbol of the Messiah Yeshua's victory is the Torah of the Spirit: our New Covenant with God that has stripped away the old nature. God made us alive along with the Messiah by forgiving us of all our sins.

Try relinquishing judgement by forgiving those who have wronged you. This is done by the Spirit. You keep putting to death the practices of the body (the old nature). This will initiate our daily walk into abundant living with the Messiah.

Read the verses from the Complete Jewish Bible (CJB) several times and see if a new perspective from our older brothers, the

Jewish people, doesn't shed new insights on our lifelong struggle with judgement.

Father, help us to see that your word has cleansed us from our old nature by bringing us in union with the Messiah Yeshua. Father, help us to destroy the power of the law with the good news of your Son's love and sacrifice. Father, I pray that we will walk in peace and joy every day. May we, your people who are called by your name, offer prayers in humility as you have asked us to do. Amen.

— *Larry Dancler, Clinical Therapist*

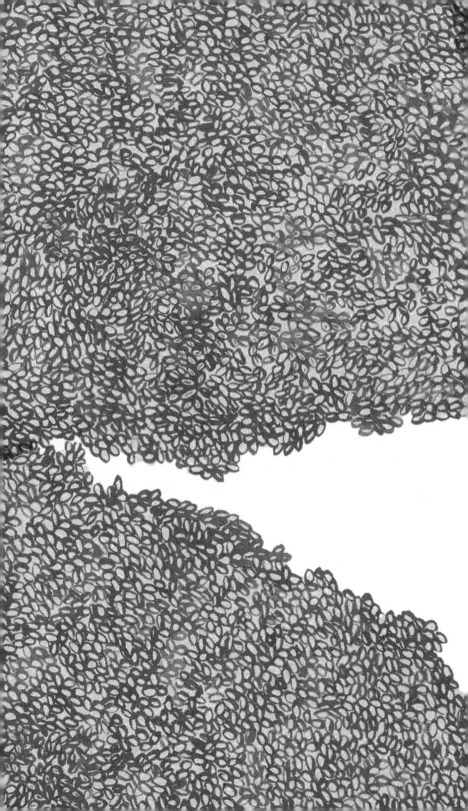

Day 23:
Freely He Relinquished Judgement
(Part Two)

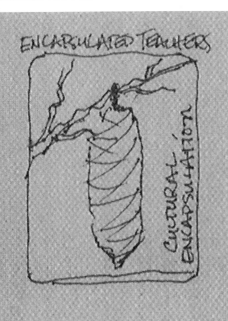

ENCAPSULATED TEACHERS

CULTURAL ENCAPSULATION

TRAUMATIZE BRAIN

TOXIC STRESS

DR. JE CHAMBERS
STRONGHOLD COUNSEL
334-7713 www.stronghold counseli

"They aren't connected anymore to the head, who is Christ. But the whole body grows from the head. The muscles and tendons hold the body together. And God causes it to grow."

— *Colossians 2:19 (NIRV)* —

FREELY HE RELINQUISHED JUDGEMENT

(PART TWO)

In one of my last conversations with JC, I asked how to respond to a particularly difficult client, working under the assumption that there was a "right" answer and it was up to me to find it. JC said that he gets lost sometimes, too. Then he pulled the pockets out of his jeans, looked up, and said, "God, I've got nothing. I need you to use me and speak through me, because I'm nothing without you." JC told me that God gave me gifts, and that I couldn't have accomplished anything on my own without Him. And he told me to trust in the Lord, and to take all things to Him.

We have education, skill, and training, but we must keep in mind that we are also human. We don't have to know it all, or do it all, and we are not alone. We can always look to Jesus for strength, wisdom, and guidance in all things. Jesus wants us to be grounded, firmly rooted in His truth, and to seek Him. We aren't expected to have all of the answers, but to seek the One who knows all things.

God, thank you for sharing your truth. Help us to discern teachings that align with your Word from the teachings of this world. Please help us to provide godly wisdom to others, while always pointing them back to you. Amen.

Dig deeper: Colossians 2:13-23

— *Amanda Davis, Clinical Therapist*

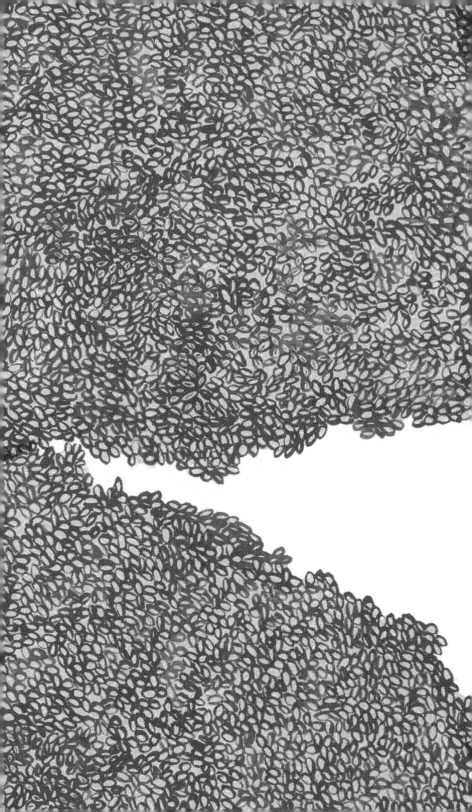

Day 24: Freely He Sent the Spirit (Part One)

"When he comes, he will show that the world is wrong about sin, about righteousness and about judgment — about sin, in that people don't put their trust in me; about righteousness, in that I am going to the Father and you will no longer see me; about judgment, in that the ruler of this world has been judged."

— John 16:8-11 (CJB) —

24

FREELY HE SENT THE SPIRIT

(PART ONE)

(The following story comes from an unnamed source about a young Russian girl.)

Anna grew up in a dysfunctional, alcoholic family and suffered abuse. At the age of 13, she was forced to live on the streets of Moscow. Anna beat the odds and survived life on the streets. She eventually found a job and a place to live. Anna even started attending a church and put her faith in Christ. However, depression continued to plague her.

I met Anna in church and started teaching her ballet, as well as studying the Bible with her. Although she has grown in faith, she has a hard time believing God loves her unconditionally, and that she doesn't have to work to earn His love.

A few weeks ago, Anna dreamed that God spoke to her. In

her dream, He told her how much He loved her and gave her a hug. Anna woke up feeling God's love and presence in her life in a new way! We are praying that this will be a real breakthrough for her. Please pray with us that Anna would own God's unconditional love for her and walk in that truth.

As He did in Anna's life, He can speak to me and you. In John 16, John tells us that the Holy Spirit's job is to come, to speak to us, and clarify things. There are three things in particular: sin, righteousness, and judgment. It seems that he is saying that the teaching that we have learned about sin, righteousness, and judgment from the world has led us astray. It seems to breed distrust and set up hostility between us and God.

Without the comforter in our lives, we cannot know that God is loving. We cannot know that Jesus sits at the right hand of the Father and freely gives us, because of where He sits, good standing with God the Father. We cannot know that the source of judgment in this world has been judged and his power to judge, to separate, to confuse, and to divide has been conquered and overthrown.

If we just trust Him, He will help us discover that He loves us, that He will hug us, that we matter to Him, and that He's committed to us. He will see us through this life and clarify the things that are divine from the things that are of this world.

Dear Father, help us to dig deeper, to understand further, and to trust more in your love, your mercy, and your grace for us, so that through us other people can know how deeply they're loved by you. Amen.

Dig deeper: John 16:5-15 and 1 Corinthians 2:9-16

— Dr. JC Chambers, Co-founder (1959-2018)

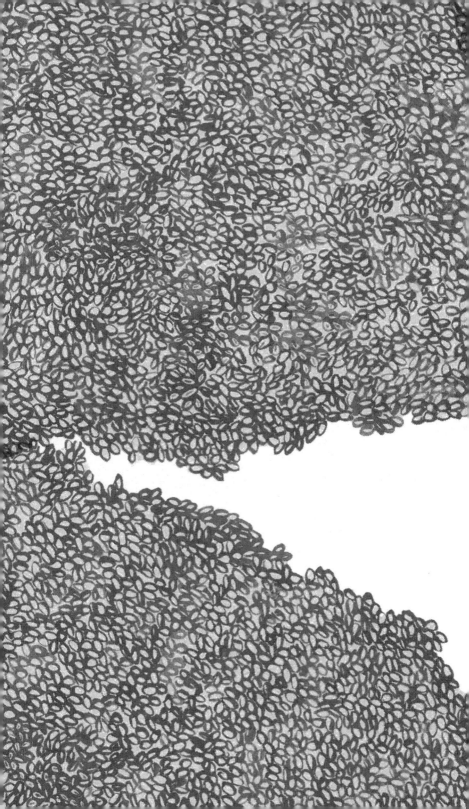

Day 25: Freely He Sent the Spirit (Part Two)

"However, as it is written: 'What no eye has seen, what no ear has heard, and what no human mind has conceived'—the things God has prepared for those who love him—these are the things God has revealed to us by his Spirit. The Spirit searches all things, even the deep things of God. For who knows a person's thoughts except their own spirit within them? In the same way no one knows the thoughts of God except the Spirit of God. What we have received is not the spirit of the world, but the Spirit who is from God, so that we may understand what God has freely given us. This is what we speak, not in words taught us by human wisdom but in words taught by the Spirit, explaining spiritual realities with Spirit-taught words. The person without the Spirit does not accept the things that come from the Spirit of God but considers them foolishness, and cannot understand them because they are discerned only through the Spirit. The person with the Spirit makes judgments about all things, but such a person is not subject to merely human judgments, for, 'Who has known the mind of the Lord so as to instruct him?' But we have the mind of Christ."

— *1 Corinthians 2:9-16 (NIV)* —

FREELY HE SENT THE SPIRIT

(PART TWO)

The Greek word used for the Holy Spirit is parakletos, meaning, "advocate, intercessor, legal assistant, called to one's aid." There is a price that was paid to have the Spirit come—Jesus' death.

Life constantly gives us a choice, such as left or right, peach or apple pie, $2000 fine or a month in jail. Sometimes we want both, sometimes neither, and sometimes the choice is made for us. We could have Jesus or the Spirit, but it was best for us to have the Spirit. Jesus said that, *"It is for your good that I am going away. Unless I go away, the Advocate will not come to you,"* John 16:7 (**NIV**).

When someone leaves us, what they leave us with is greater than when they were with us. They become bigger in their death than they were in life; they multiply. It is never a good time, and we always want more of these individuals who leave their mark on us. However, God wants what is best for us. It was good to have Jesus, but it was better for Him to leave so that the Spirit may come and we may understand God more.

Father, I don't know the reason why you do what you do. I don't know what the future holds, but I know who holds the future. Thank you for your Spirit, who allows me to walk with you in an intimate way. May I learn to lean into, rather than away from, what you have in store for me. Lead me by your Spirit to have the mind of Christ. Amen.

— *Earl Witt, Clinical Therapist*

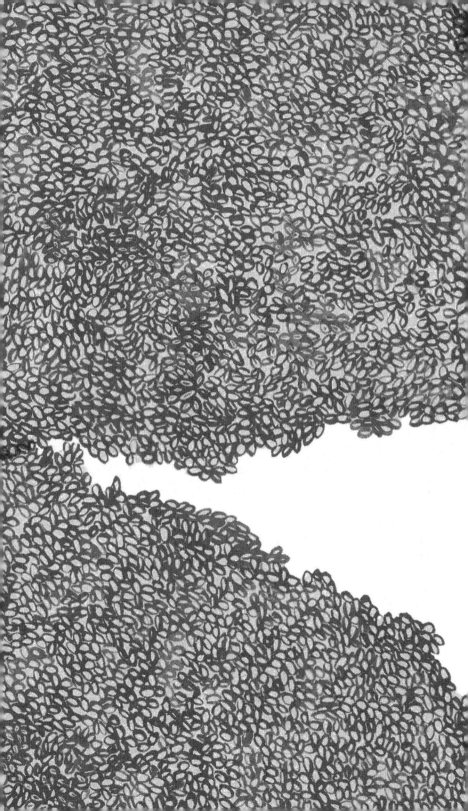

Day 26: Freely We Approach

(8/3/17)

"JUST MERCY"
AMAZING
STUFF TO
CONSIDER

Generate More Ideas
Generate More Approaches
Some will SUCK guaranteed
But you'll find a Diamond too
On the to Diamonds you'll throw
Away lots of Rocks...

"FAMILY"
CHOSSEN, BROUGHT IN
"We're His Ambassadors"

"THA ROCK that
CAUSES MEN to
STUMBLE &
FALL"

"JESUS"
"THA GOSPEL"

"ANGRY Father's
LINE"

REFLECT THA SON!!

"To improve is to change... ...ious is to change often." WINSTON CHURCHILL

"Therefore, since we have a great high priest who has ascended into heaven, Jesus the Son of God, let us hold firmly to the faith we profess. For we do not have a high priest who is unable to empathize with our weaknesses, but we have one who has been tempted in every way, just as we are—yet he did not sin. Let us then approach God's throne of grace with confidence, so that we may receive mercy and find grace to help us in our time of need."

— Hebrews 4:14-16 (NIV) —

FREELY WE APPROACH

Therefore. We have heard these things, and now an action must be taken in thought and in heart.

Therefore. An in-between word so simple that we might almost miss it. The word is nudged between the already and the call of what is to come. It is a word that often means there are implications for what we've already been told. It's a word which indicates some sort of consequence or end result of something happening. Therefore is a transition. It is a space that simply is, until what follows it is written on the page.

On July 8, 2018 my dad died due to a bilateral pulmonary embolism, taking his life way too soon. Therefore. Therefore, my mom, my sisters, and myself are left without a husband, without a dad. Therefore, we grieve. Therefore, we stand in confusion, anger, and madness without any sort of sense of what has happened. We are still living with the blow of the aftermath of his death. The shock of my dad's death rings so loudly in all of our lives, that we stand in this in-between space waiting for the words, the meaning, the sense behind it all, that might, or might not, come. Right now we stand in the "therefore." We stand in the aftermath of death, waiting for something. We stand in a space that is; a space that on it's own has neither an end nor a beginning, a purpose or a meaning, but it just simply is.

For the recipients of this letter to the Hebrews, being in the space of the therefore meant being in a space of persecution due to their faith in Christ. They stood with the already, a promised faith and religion that offered them the way to salvation but was in reality offering them suffering and hardship. They stood waiting for the offering of what is to come after the therefore. And here, in Hebrews 4:14-16, they get their therefore.

The author lays out beforehand the premise, the basis of the gospel—Jesus Christ's superiority over all the priests and prophets and leaders of the faith. The basis of the gospel that promises that Christ is who scripture claims Him to be. Just verses before, the author lays out the stronghold that the word of God has on our lives. The word of God is alive and active. The word of God is energetic. The word of God is powerful, and its promises are true.

Therefore. Here, the therefore invites the Hebrews into an

action because of what is said to be true about Jesus Christ, the great high priest who was fully human, and freely given as the merciful, suffering savior who knows the pain and persecution that the Hebrews faced.

Christ was tempted and engaged in the full scope of human weakness and knows our deepest hurt and pain. Therefore. Therefore in grief, in mourning, in a space that feels overwhelming, vast, and sad, we can freely approach the throne of grace with confidence that our Lord knows and understands our grief.

If we believe God to be who God says he is—a God who freely gives, freely comes, freely reconciles, freely loves, freely suffered, freely redeems, freely grants peace, freely sent the spirit, freely waits, freely forgets, freely relinquished judgment, freely enters our mourning, and freely extends righteousness— then the invitation for us in Hebrews is the freedom to enter God's presence in confidence, even as we struggle to make sense of the tragedy and pain in our lives. Even when we are so angry all we can do is yell. Even when our hearts are so shattered that we can't make sense of our faith. Even when we are so confused that we don't know what to believe about faith.

The invitation in Hebrews, the claim to hold firm to the faith we profess is an invitation to remember we have a high priest who knows our pain intimately. Freely, we can approach the presence of God, bringing with us the full scope of our pain and anger, our sorrows, and the broken pieces of our hearts.

I know that God can handle the rage I feel from the death of my dad. I still stand in the therefore, a space that is painful and hard. Yet I find moments to step into the healing that comes in moments of freely offering my whole, angry, sad, confused, grieving heart to the great high priest.

Father, freely, we have received all of these promises and truths about a God who freely is. Therefore, freely, we offer ourselves. Freely, we approach. Freely, we pray. Freely, we mourn. Freely, we grieve. Help us to freely find healing at your grace-filled throne. Amen.

— Haley Chambers Wiggers

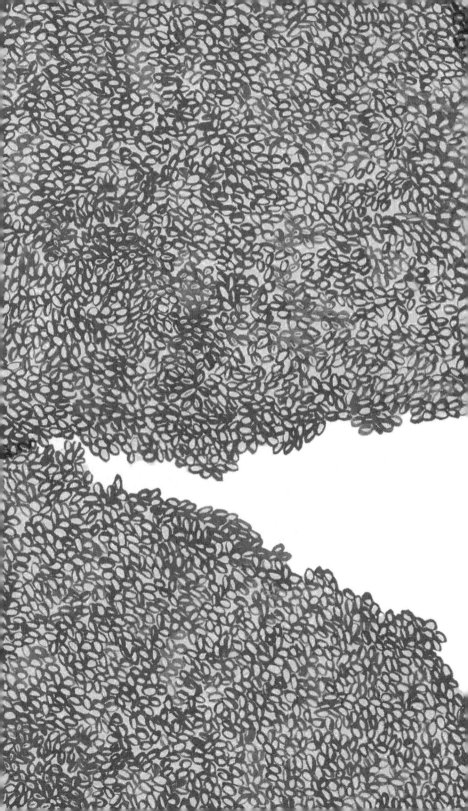

Day 27: Freely He Enters Our Mourning (Part One)

"Jesus wept."

— John 11:35 (NIV) —

FREELY HE ENTERS OUR MOURNING

(PART ONE)

Those are two simple words, and yet they hold an incredible amount of significance that only He could share.

When Jesus saw the grief of the family and friends who were mourning the death of Lazarus, He wept. Jesus wept, not because He lacked faith, for He knew God's plan to resurrect Lazarus. He wept because of His deep compassion and love for those who were suffering. *"When Jesus saw her weeping, and the Jews who had come with her also weeping, He was deeply moved in His spirit and greatly troubled,"* John 11:33.

When someone we love dies, we are heartbroken and our tears flow. Our loss may leave us feeling distraught and overwhelmed. It may feel like nobody can understand our pain, our emptiness, and our sadness. But Jesus, in His humanity, felt within

His body and spirit the emotional pain of love, sadness, disappointment, loss, and grief of Lazarus' friends and family. He was moved to tears. Tears that speak so much more than words.

Washington Irving's quote sheds a unique light on the meaning of tears: "There is a sacredness in tears. They are not the mark of weakness, but of power. They speak more eloquently than ten thousand tongues. They are the messengers of overwhelming grief, of deep contrition, and of unspeakable love."

Jesus wept just like we do when we feel the sting of death. He meets us at our pain, not to take away our tears, but to hold us and comfort us as we mourn the loss of someone we love. At times, the most powerful response to sorrow is not in words. It's an emotional response—the "unspeakable love" that comes from the depth of the heart's emotion.

Jesus understands what we are going through. His tears give us permission to shed our own tears. We are never alone in our pain. He is always with us. Although we mourn the loss of a loved one who we will dearly miss, we can stand firmly in the promise of the resurrection.

"Blessed are those who mourn, for they will be comforted," Matthew 5:4.

Dear Father, we thank you for holding us close as we mourn those precious to us. We are grateful that we can reach out to you for comfort and peace as you truly understand our deepest pain. Guide us as we show compassion for others who are grieving and share our love in both words and tears. Help us to love as deeply as you, trusting in your word and keeping our hearts and minds on the resurrection and life to come. Amen.

— Myra Heckenlaible-Gotto, Former Clinical Therapist

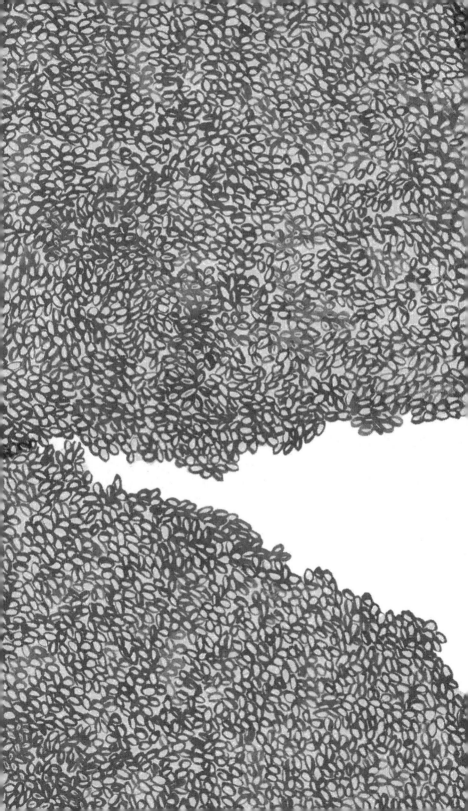

Day 28: Freely He Enters Our Mourning (Part Two)

"Jesus wept."

— *John 11:35 (NIV)* —

FREELY HE ENTERS OUR MOURNING

(PART TWO)

The verse I picked is about Jesus entering our mourning. I chose this because I have been drowning in mourning for about 6 weeks now. Before my dad died, the only things dear to me that had passed away were two beloved dogs. I had never experienced this kind of loss and unrelenting, searing pain. Before, I couldn't relate to people who had endured something like this. It's unexplainable how quickly sadness envelops your life. Every night I pray that I will dream about him so that I can see him and talk to him. Every morning I wake up and remember that he is gone. I find myself constantly wiping the tears away and swallowing the lump that creeps up in the back of my throat when I'm thinking about him, talking about him, listening to a song he loved, designing, painting, watching basketball, or doing any of those things we had in common that we both loved to do.

Last week I saw a man mildly resembling my dad wearing a "Jesus Rocks" shirt and a ball cap, and I seriously contemplated asking the man to hug me. Am I losing it? Maybe. Am I mad at God? Kinda. Do I still have faith? I think so. My dad told me a long time ago that anger is never the primary emotion, but that there is usually some other emotion behind it. So when I say "mad" at God, I mostly mean I am devastated. I am devastated about Him getting to have my dad, while I'm left here without him.

"Find comfort in knowing he's with Jesus," they say. "Rejoice, he's in Heaven," they tell me. Well, to be quite honest, I'm not rejoicing. I am a little miffed. I am here, left on this earth, and probably will be for a while.

But you know what? God doesn't care that I am mad at Him. He knows the root reasons. He knows I miss my dad. He knows exactly how I feel and why I cry every day. He understands the pain. Jesus wept, too. He didn't just watch suffering from the sidelines. He felt it. He ugly cried. I mean, the text does say "wept," not just "shed tears." Jesus freely wept, and so do I. Someday I will probably weep less, but for now, I mourn. I weep. And it's ok.

Dear Jesus, I know this will not be the only uphill battle I have to face during my time here on Earth. But I know you still hold me in your hands during this season of mourning. Thank you for getting me through each of these difficult days. Amen.

— *Carley Chambers Childs*

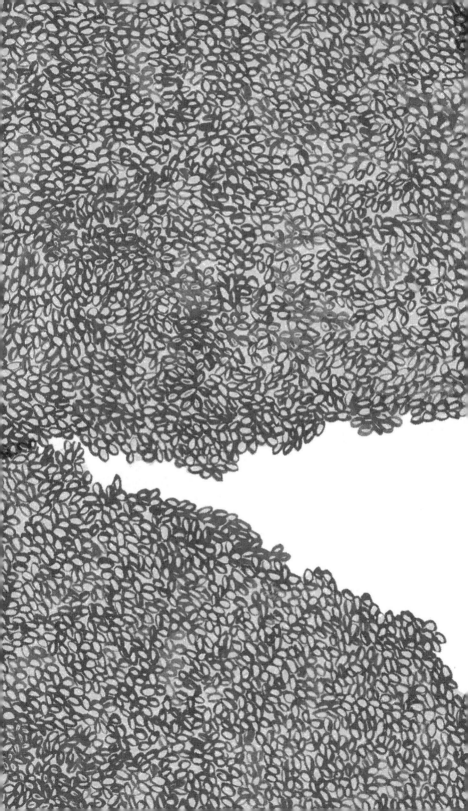

Day 29: Freely He Enters Our Mourning (Part Three)

"Jesus wept."

— *John 11:35 (NIV)* —

29

FREELY HE ENTERS OUR MOURNING

(PART THREE)

There is a list in front of you. You are free to choose anything on that list, but you must choose a certain set amount from each section on the list. Included throughout the sections are getting married, buying a house, having children, losing a job, losing a child, having wonderful friends, getting in a car accident, having enough food on the table all your life, living to be old, dying young, being healthy, etc. Such things all make up life. But in this scenario, you must choose a few things from each section on the list and that is what your life will be like. My children and I talked about this when they were younger. We didn't know if we would want to know what our life was going to consist of. Would you? Would you freely choose a manger over a castle, being born to a young mother, being thought of as a bastard all your life, being rejected by family and friends? Would you choose waiting and watching a best friend named Lazarus die when you had the power to stop it? I don't think I would. In fact, I hated that game when my kids and I would play it in the car. I didn't want to think about knowing the pain that was inevitably coming my way. There are some things you just can't prepare for. Ease makes less of an impression on us than struggles. Yet we will avoid the struggles at all costs. Jesus didn't. Jesus entered this life, and He enters our lives. The saying goes, "pain shared is halved, joy shared is doubled." Jesus freely entered into life, pain, and our mourning. And when He enters, He wants to take all of it, not just half.

Jesus, you understand us better than we understand ourselves. You understand our pain and endured so much for us. Thank you!

— *Gena Tarrell, Office Manager*

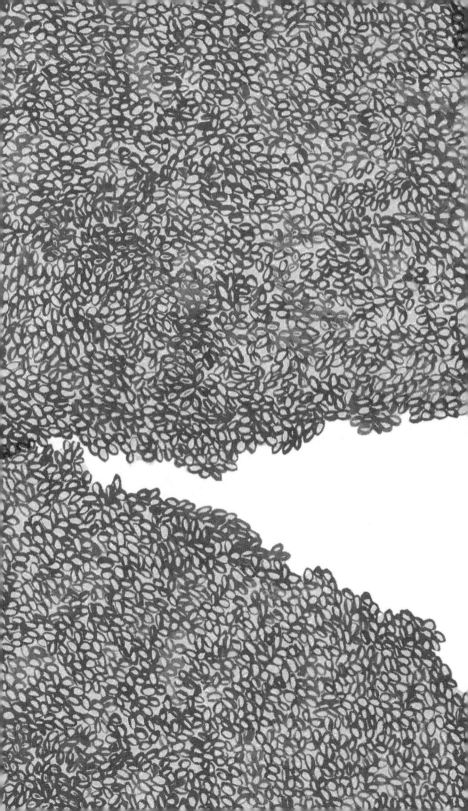

Day 30: Freely He Will Reconcile

"THE RESURRECTION STORY LIVES"

"We are Christ's ambassadors. God is using us to speak to you: we beg you, as though Christ himself were here pleading with you, receive the love he offers you—be reconciled to God."

— 2 Corinthians 5:20 (TLB) —

FREELY HE WILL RECONCILE

Reconciling is a big word, but its meaning is contained in three small words. It means "to make right." How that's done can be an interesting story, though. I am the mother-in-love of Jay Chambers, and our story of reconciliation shows confession, forgiveness, grace, and lots of love.

Go back to 1982. Life in a small, Middle American community was pretty simple. We lived and worked on a dairy farm, and we were all active in our church. The kids learned responsibility through chores and 4-H. All five of them were active in sports and academically inclined. We were the normal family, and our new home was dedicated and open to whoever the Lord sent our way, and we hosted many international kids and families. I wouldn't have considered myself prejudiced in any way. We loved the Lord and were serving Him in our church and in our community.

On Thanksgiving one year, my college-aged daughter showed up late for dinner with three of her friends. One was a tall, gangly, good-looking black basketball player, who I soon came to realize was going to be my enemy if he pursued my daughter. They fell in love and I fell apart. I had nothing against African-Americans, but in that day, in my world, I didn't think interracial marriage was okay, even between believers. So I quoted scripture verses, took away my daughter's car and even made sarcastic racial slurs. I was awful. I basically told him to break off his relationship with my daughter. I felt like a mama bear fighting for her youngest child, as I loved her very much and their relationship was tearing apart the closeness we had always had.

Despite all this, Jay never said anything bad to me, but we kept our distance. I prayed without ceasing and made deals with God, asking, "If you stop this relationship, I will never ask another thing from you." The funny thing is, though, God knew me and still said no. They were married while he was attending NAB Seminary, and she continued school in South Dakota. When they got married, I thought my heart was broken. I was at the bottom of a pit. I was depressed, crushed, and I didn't know if life was worth living.

When you finally reach the end of your pride is when God can really start working. I started listening to what He wanted instead of what I wanted. Reconciliation begins with tears, regret, confession, and a changing of your heart. Fortunately, God was already one step ahead. Jay and I began to have conversations. He was ready to forgive me when I asked him to. He was kind and gracious, even though I didn't deserve it.

So it is with God giving us grace and reconciliation when we don't deserve it. He is ready to listen, and He patiently beckons us to Him. We can be reconciled to God because of Jesus. Can any of us fully realize what that means? If God cares so much about family relationships, how much more does He care about reconciling His children for eternity? The stakes of not "making it right" with God are high. So why not get it settled now? As today's verse says, listen to God's gentle voice. He beckons to you. Where will you spend eternity? Freely, He offers reconciliation. All we need to do is accept it.

Jay was a continued blessing to our family, and he was loved by all of us. It's too bad I wasted some of the time I could have spent with him. Use the time you have left getting to know Jesus. He calls to you with a redeeming love that makes right our connection with Him.

Father, thank you for the grace you give us, even when we don't deserve it. You are faithful and forgive us and promise us a life reconciled to you for all eternity. All we have to do is take the gift you freely offer. Amen.

Dig deeper: 2 Corinthians 5:17-21

— *Marian DeWerff*

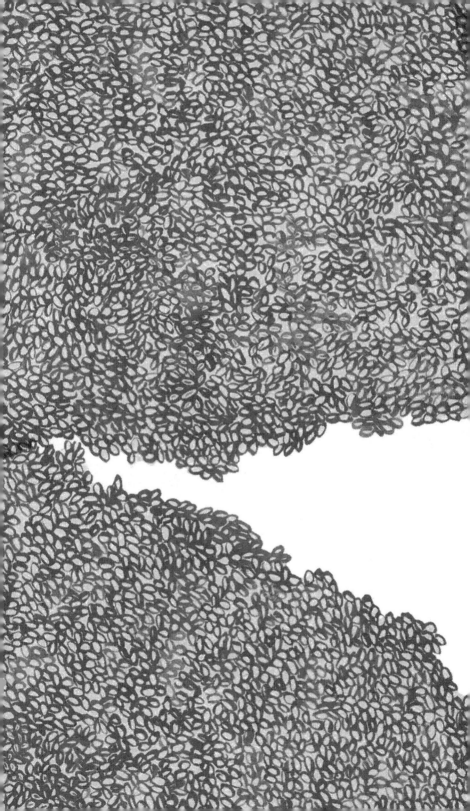

About the Author

FREELY

ABOUT THE AUTHOR

Jamie Christopher (JC) Chambers, born December 8, 1959, died unexpectedly while doing one of the things he loved most—coaching girls basketball, on Sunday, July 8, 2018. JC was born in Denver, Colorado and was lovingly raised by his Grandmother Dorothy Thomas. He attended Regis High School in Denver and went to play basketball and attend school as an Art Education and Psychology major at Sterling College in Sterling, KS where he received his BA in 1983. While at Sterling, he met Lorri DeWerff and they were married in 1984. He received his Masters in Counseling at North American Baptist Seminary in Sioux Falls, SD in 1985. He immediately began a Doctoral program at the University of South Dakota and graduated in 1992 with an Ed.D in Counselor Education. He then became a Licensed Psychologist and Marital and Family Therapist with special interest in at-risk youth, marriage, families, and chemical dependency.

Following a near-death experience in 1993, JC felt called to start a grace-based counseling practice in Sioux Falls called Stronghold Counseling Services, named after Proverbs 18:10, "The name of the LORD is a strong tower; the righteous run into it and are safe." His partnership with co-founder Marlene Ruff lasted until 2003 when he became sole owner.

JC felt passionate about helping people find hope in seemingly hopeless circumstances and leading people to grace that is found in Jesus Christ. This grace was the basis for all that he did, and it was evident in the way he loved, parented, coached, mentored, and worked. If he wasn't working or with his family, he was coaching basketball. If he wasn't coaching, he was fly-fishing in the Black Hills of South Dakota. And if he wasn't fly-fishing, he was creating works of art, or making music.

JC was an artist, in what he created with his hands, the ways he loved people, and mostly the ways he loved the Lord. His bookshelves are filled with pages of sketches and drawings of anything that came to his mind, such as basketball plays, practice plans, sermon ideas, and brilliant pictures of what he imagined Jesus to look like. His writing led him to publish two books: "The Art of Kid Whispering," and "The Stronghold Difference." His books and work as a counselor revealed his heart, wisdom, and ability to foster authentic transformation.

His hands created instruments, pieces of art, and sunk many free throws in his lifetime. He showed up in people's lives in the exact way they needed and carried each person's heart with compassion. Most importantly, he lived and died as a servant of God, supporting his family, playing drums, singing hip-hop, writing devotions, coaching and mentoring everyone's children all for the glory of his Creator.

True to the form of a servant leader, even after his death, the mission he started endures. Stronghold Counseling continues to serve those who are hurting, lost, or seeking to improve their life. While JC cannot be seen everyday at Stronghold as he once was, his presence is still certainly felt.

ABOUT THE AUTHOR

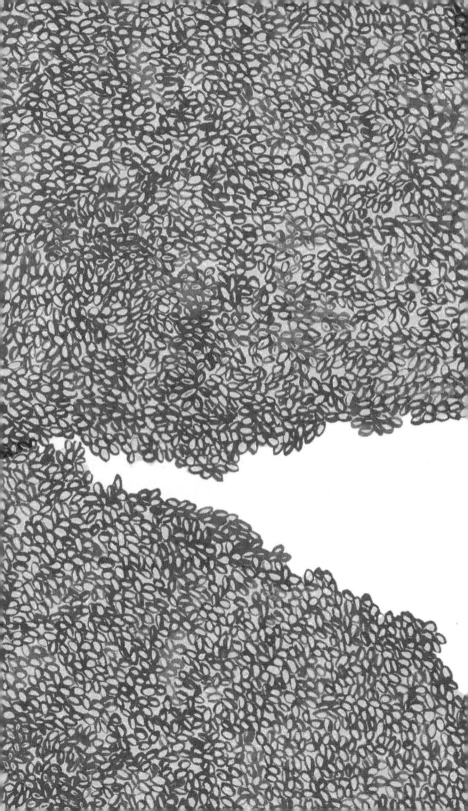

About Stronghold Counseling Services (The Crew)

ABOUT STRONGHOLD COUNSELING SERVICES

(THE CREW)

Our Mission

"The name of the LORD is a strong tower; the righteous run to it and are safe." Proverbs 18:10 (NKJV)

Stronghold started as a vision of founding partners J.C. Chambers, Ed.D., and Marlene Ruff, M.A., as a place where those who are hurting could experience both clinical excellence and God's grace. There are certainly many fine treatment centers specializing in traditional clinical care, along with several outstanding Christian based counseling services. However, we find the combination of these two healing approaches to be unique.

The mission of Stronghold is to dispense God's grace in reaching those outside the church door, while providing services that are clinically astute, sound, and at the highest level of excellence. Stronghold is not in the business of preaching, judging, or proselytizing. Stronghold is about healing. The kind of deep healing that happens when therapy resides on the spiritual level, addressing all the elements that make up the whole person.

The Stronghold Difference

Stronghold was created in 1993 to offer hope; the hope of real healing for those hurting in a broken world. Healing never takes place alone. Many times it is the result of deliberate, intentional, caring service from committed professionals with years of experience, such as professional counselors who have already helped hundreds in similar situations. This hope is the foundation of the Stronghold experience.

Hope Without Hype

Healing is never easy. There is no quick fix. It is often painful. It does not happen overnight. But real, life-changing healing can and does happen, regardless of what often may seem like a mountain of overwhelming circumstances. True, we don't know what you're going through. But at Stronghold, you'll never have to face it alone.

Guidance Without Judgement

Stronghold was founded on a philosophy of non-judgmental counseling. Before healing can happen, open communication must take place in a safe environment free of judgment. Stronghold provides a "judgment-free" zone where individuals and families can honestly open up, often for the first time without any fear of repercussions.

Contact Stronghold Counseling Services, Inc.

Website: StrongholdCounseling.com
Email: info@strongholdcounseling.com
Phone For All Locations: (605) 334-7713
Fax: (605) 334-5348

Address:
Sioux Falls Location:
4300 S Louise Ave, Suite 201
Sioux Falls, SD 57106

Yankton Location:
610 W 23rd St #8
Yankton, SD 57078

Spearfish Location:
1320 North Ave
Spearfish, SD 57783

"A House on the Rock"

"HOPE WITHOUT HYPE, GUIDANCE WITHOUT JUDGMENT"

STRONGHOLD COUNSELING SERVICES, INC

ABOUT STRONGHOLD COUNSELING SERVICES (THE CREW)

10082474R00138

Made in the USA
Lexington, KY
18 September 2018